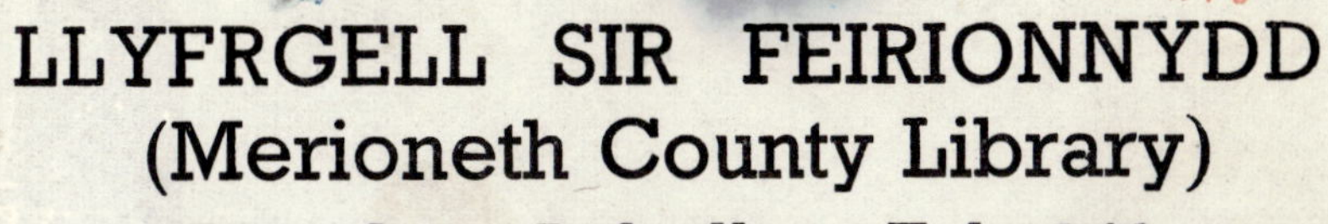

THE FRIENDLY ISLANDERS

THE FRIENDLY ISLANDERS

by

KENNETH BAIN

A story of Queen Salote and her people

With a Foreword by

HIS MAJESTY KING TAUFA'AHAU TUPOU IV

HODDER AND STOUGHTON

First published July 1967
Second impression July 1967

SBN 340 02560 3

PRINTED IN GREAT BRITAIN FOR HODDER AND STOUGHTON LIMITED, ST. PAUL'S HOUSE, WARWICK LANE, LONDON, E.C.4 BY C. TINLING AND CO. LIMITED, LIVERPOOL, LONDON AND PRESCOT

For ‘ATU, ASHLEY and VIVIAN,

whose country Tonga partly is

ACKNOWLEDGEMENTS

I am indebted to His Majesty King Taufa'ahau Tupou IV for kindness in reading the manuscript, tolerance in sanctioning its appearance and generosity in writing the Foreword; also to Fiji Public Relations Officer Jack Hackett, for the official photographs by Rob Wright and Rob Wright Jnr.; and to the Controller of H.M. Stationery Office, London, for allowing me to draw on articles of mine published in *Corona* magazine.

With the agreement of the Government of Tonga, I have also included three short passages, the substance of which appeared in my *Royal Visit to Tonga*, Pitkin, 1954.

Suva, KENNETH BAIN
Fiji,
1st June 1966

Contents

The Plates

[1] Syndication International.
[2] *Auckland Star*.
[3] Tevita Vaka, Tonga Government Official Photographer.

Foreword

This book contains legends and many interesting and amusing stories about Tonga and the Tongans such as came within the knowledge and experience of the author. It ends with a tragic occurrence, but human life must be expected to contain both happiness and sadness.

Tonga, of course, has changed in many ways since the author was stationed there. The radio and newspaper, together with better surface and air communications with the outside world, have reduced the feeling of isolation and have increased the awareness of new economic opportunities opening up. Tongan growers of produce, for example, watch the price of produce in neighbouring territories as keenly as the American farmer would watch the commodities futures market in Chicago. However, dealings are confined to concrete commodities presently available—which is just as well.

It is true that Tongans have trouble with time, but perhaps this is natural owing to the fact that Tongan civil time is calculated on two different meridians and not on one. The days of the week are calculated on 180 degrees so that the same days are maintained as in Australia, New Zealand, Fiji and other countries of the Eastern Hemisphere. The hours of the day are based on 165 degrees west longitude. Instead of Tongan time being 11 hours behind G.M.T., it is 13 hours ahead.

So here, as in many other ways, Tonga is always trying to get the best of both worlds—or all worlds if there are more than two. All this tends to confuse strangers, but it is the normal Tongan way of life!

TAUFA'AHAU TUPOU

The Palace,
Nuku'alofa,
TONGA.
27th July, 1966.

Preface

CONTEMPORARY Tonga is a study of custom in transition. It has the trappings of a modern constitutional government in a Christian state; and it may now be on the brink of the great tourism breakthrough. Side by side is a semi-feudal social structure, with traditional obligations and inhibitions, the origins of which are lost in the shadows of the past. The structure is complete and self-contained. The non-Tongan fits in as best he can.

Superimposed on this is a history of battle and bloodshed leading to the acceptance of Christianity, and of sectarian bitterness and fragmentation thereafter. The emotions aroused in the early days of Christian evangelism are still reflected today in parts of the Tongan law. Add the racial traits and pride of the Polynesian, and you have an intricate social and national pattern.

The executive machinery of the Tonga Government has not yet reconciled what some regard as the irreconcilable; and the stranger can be confused and frustrated by difficulties he does not understand and which may never be adequately explained to him. It is easy to criticise the ineptitude of others when you have neither responsibility for decision nor understanding of the processes which lead to it. It is tempting to dismiss the unfamiliar as wrong; and to regard subjectively conditioned standards as sacrosanct. To do so in Polynesia is to fall into error.

This book is neither an anthropological study nor a comprehensive analysis of present-day Tonga. If it reflects the many faces of Tonga, it could be read as a cautionary tale for young administrators, as I was, and for superficial commentators, which I hope I am not.

If I have laughed, I would wish to have laughed with the Tongans and not at them. For, had it not been for their innate sense of dignity and restraint, they would have had occasion to laugh, many a time, at me.

I In the Beginning

IN the dim far-distant days of the past, Tongamatamoana was the great god of the heavens and his only daughter lived as one of the earthly creatures below. As the god's daughter grew to womanhood, she became as beautiful as any star in the universe; and to preserve her from earthly danger, Tongamatamoana took her away from the earth to the sky where she could enjoy his protection. So that the risk of earthly intrusion should be slight, the great god made to his house a hazardous pathway and few there were with knowledge of its beginning.

When her friends of the earth came to know that the girl had vanished, they searched in every village in every land. But they could find no trace of her. Then it was that the priests said that she had returned to the sky, since she was of the gods and not of worldly men. The young men of the village sought to find and traverse the road to the heavens to bring back the beautiful maiden they had lost. None succeeded; for all who made the attempt died on the way and did not return and no one could find the reason.

At last there were but two left who would make the attempt: the fishermen, Maui Kisikisi and his brother Maui 'Atalanga. Together they set out to face the wrath of the god and make their way to the girl's heavenly home. When they had found the place at which the path began, their way was easy until they passed Pulotu, where the spirits of the dead leave this world for the spirit world beyond. Soon, however, they were bewildered and lost and were unable to perceive which way to continue.

Maui 'Atalanga said, "Let us stay here awhile so that we shall find someone who will be able to tell us which way we should take; for I fear that if we do not do so, we may meet our death as have our brothers before us."

So Maui Kisikisi and Maui 'Atalanga waited by the side of the road and, as the day drew to its close, they saw in the distance the figure of a woman coming towards them. Observing that she was a goddess, the two brothers, though in great fear, resolved to speak to her. "O great one of the sky, is this the way which leads to the home of Tongamatamoana and his daughter?" they asked.

"Yes," the woman replied, "the road lies ahead."

"But how may we reach the heavens," they asked, "for we have heard that many have died on the way?"

"If you have good heart and take heed of what I tell you," said the goddess, "you will be safe and will find what you seek. If you do not, then you too will die and the daughter of Tongamatamoana will forever remain beyond the sight of earthly men."

"Pray tell us," they beseeched her, "and we shall obey."

"Then follow me," said the woman, "and do as I say."

So they started on their journey once more. After they had been walking for many hours and were growing cold and hungry, the woman turned to them and said:

"A short distance from this spot you will find the most succulent food set on the roadside. Since I can read what is in your minds and in your hearts, I know that you are nearly dead from hunger for you have not eaten for many hours. Should you touch or eat anything, you will die and your spirits will wander forever in the torment of the underworld below Pulotu. If you can resist the temptation to eat, you will live to continue your journey."

Presently the two brothers began to smell the aromas of roast pig, and fish of the sea and fowls of the air. As they turned a corner they saw, as she had promised, row upon row of choice delicacies set on banana leaves at the edge of the road. Exhausted from hunger and in great distress as they were, they determined to follow her instructions and began to go past the food. Then Maui 'Atalanga stopped and made move to taste it, his patience and strength at an end; but Maui Kisikisi put out his hand to his brother and together they went on their journey, their hunger unsatisfied.

In a while, they forgot their hunger and once again ahead of them they saw the goddess waiting and smiling at them.

"Well done," she said, "you have proved yourselves worthy to continue your quest."

When they had gone on a little further, the way suddenly narrowed into a hollow tunnel so tiny that they could not pass through it. "Do not take offence," said their companion, "if I strike you; for I must now change you from your human shape into something smaller."

With that, she hit them both on the head. At once they were changed into cats and so could pass through the tunnel. Then the path became still narrower. Once again the woman touched them on the head. They were changed into rats and so could continue. Although in great fear that they would never return to their earthly bodies, the two brothers took courage to continue their journey and were astonished to find the path becoming wide again. They themselves were no longer cats or rats, but men.

Soon they entered a village of fine houses, green grass and trees.

"You have done well," said their companion. "There is the house for which you are searching." And with that she left them and was not seen again.

Overjoyed at their good fortune, Maui Kisikisi and Maui 'Atalanga approached the house of Tongamatamoana and were greeted by the girl for whom they had come.

"You are welcome in my father's house," she said, "for the heavenly road is hard and narrow and many there are who have failed on the way."

When they had been given food and water, Maui Kisikisi explained that the second reason for their journey was to acquire a fish hook with the power to draw up land from the ocean; for they had heard that the great god Tongamatamoana was the possessor of such hooks.

"When my father comes back," said the girl, "you may tell him what you seek. He will invite you to examine his fish hooks and may even offer you whichever one you choose. I advise you to ignore the many fine hooks in his collection and to ask him for a small rusty hook which you will see together with the others. Even though it looks weak and old, it is this hook alone which has strength to do what you want."

Tongamatamoana returned to the house for his evening meal and the two brothers placed their request before him. They explained that the worldly place in which they lived was now too small for the many people who dwelt there and more land was needed. When the meal was over, the god and the brothers went to look at Tongamatamoana's collection of fish hooks. At once they saw that what his daughter had told them was true. There among many fine shining hooks was one which was rusted and dirty. Trusting the words of the girl, they asked the god if they might have it.

"Very well," said Tongamatamoana, "you shall have this hook, for I have heard of your courage in finding your way here and I believe you both to be brave and honest. Although it looks so poor, this is a sacred hook which is not to be given to ordinary men. Go now; and when you draw up your land from the bottomless depths of the ocean with this hook, you shall call it Tongatapu or sacred Tonga."

So Maui Kisikisi and Maui ʻAtalanga returned to the earth and one day, as they fished in the waters of the ocean with the sacred hook granted to them by the great god of the sky, they pulled up the island of Tongatapu from the bottom of the sea. Then they went further and drew up Haʻapai and Vavaʻu and other smaller islands, all of which together they called Tonga after the god who had endowed the earth with this new and holy land.

And that is how the islands of Tonga arose from the ocean as part of the earth world.

2 A Drive in the Rain

THE voyage had been mercifully short—only thirty-six hours from Suva to Nuku'alofa after one of those frantic surges through space from London. The wartime freighter *Waikawa* fell somewhat below the luxury class of shipboard travel. There were eight passengers, all of whom—apart from myself—had embarked in Sydney and were bound for Vancouver. The only hoped-for relief from the tedium of each other's company during the ship's wallowing progress across the Pacific was the prospect of Bastille Day in Tahiti. Strong and regular pressure was applied to the ship's officers to ensure the success of the delaying tactics which were essential in Nuku'alofa if the ship were not to arrive and depart from the harbour of Papeete before the excitements began.

Apart from a daily airing of this tantalising topic, there was little on the ship to excite comment. She was under Canadian articles and was, we found, dry. We were served with vast quantities of lime juice with every meal, breakfast not excepted; and my fellow passengers had apparently come to accept the barbarous meal hours which the New Zealand members of the crew curiously insisted was the result of sailing under 'foreign' rules Curiously, since its meal hours are one of the trials of the New Zealand way of life.

Breakfast was from seven-thirty to eight a.m., lunch from eleven-thirty to noon and dinner, or high tea as I suppose it was, between five-thirty and six p.m. From then on, we played dominoes on top of my trunks and boxes which occupied a goodly part of the bird-cage lounge. At about seven-thirty p.m. the passengers succumbed to social suffocation and went to bed. To my relief, I was committed to a sentence of only two nights.

An hour out from Tongatapu, we seemed to be in mid-ocean. Then a flat smudge of coconut palms began to grow out of the sea.

Soon this was surmounted in part by a line of stately Norfolk pines flanking the sea shore. Through the leaves and branches glinted the white walls of Queen Salote's Palace and Royal Chapel. The Tongan Royal Standard floated from the Palace tower. Further along the shore, the Union Jack marked the British Residency. I was about to transfer for three years from British Colonial Service via Canadian to Tongan articles. The latter quickly revealed themselves in an unexpected light.

I was to succeed Atwell Lake, an Old Etonian bachelor with a drily discerning wit and a predilection for midnight debate. He met me on the ship and we went ashore with my bags to the Customs shed. There was no other landing passenger. The officer in charge approached and Atwell introduced us.

"Yes, we knew you were coming. I am glad to welcome you to Tonga. I hope I can help to make your stay a happy one."

Now this, I thought, was really something. The Customs officers of the Friendly Islands did not appear to belong to the same club as some I had met elsewhere.

"Well, yes, you can—by clearing my baggage, thank you."

"Oh, I don't mean that, Bain. I am your relation and it is my duty to look after you. So if you have any trouble just let me know and I will fix it."

There were times when I did have need of his assistance. He did just as he had promised, but he never revealed the basis of his claim of family kinship. It did not seem to matter.

Atwell and I were sitting on the verandah of his house before dinner that evening. The housekeeper, a somewhat formidable matriarch, emerged from the kitchen and said abruptly:

"Leiki"—she pronounced it Leh-ee-kee—"your dinner's ready. Can I bring it now?"

He nodded and we sat down to eat. When she had gone, I asked him to give me lesson number one in Tongan etiquette and mode of address.

"You must understand," he said, "that Tongan titles of nobility and chiefliness require no honorific or prefix. For example, it is perfectly proper to refer to 'Ulukalala or 'Aku'ola or 'Ata—all nobles—simply by their title. It is much the same as the titles of

Scottish chieftains. You will be addressed many times as you have been today by the Customs officer."

So it was that I was often addressed simply as "Bain" or "Peini", the latter being my surname in the Tongan language.

After dinner, the housekeeper brought in a shy little Tongan boy. "Young Leiki wishes to say goodnight to you," she said.

I pondered over the nature of the establishment which had been kept by my predecessor.

He smiled. "No, you are wrong. She has a child whom she has named after me, in the Tongan version. That's all. It is quite a common custom."

This explanation seemed very dubious to me, but my education was just beginning.

It had all started when I saw my name on the OHMS envelope as I passed the notice board. As it was just inside the club entrance, we always looked there as we passed for evidence of any interest by our far-off masters. Over the years, the stamps of fifty Colonial territories had appeared on the board—Nigeria, the Gold Coast, Kenya, Tanganyika, Uganda, Northern Rhodesia, Malaya, Sarawak, Jamaica, Fiji—the lot. It was May 1953 and the Colonial Service Club relaxed in the genial sunshine of an early Oxford summer.

In the lounge, a Zanzibari debated a point of classical Arabic with an Aden Arab. They both spoke in English. A Trinidad wife, enveloped in green, knitted in a corner. Tea cups and needles clicked in unison; a Provincial Commissioner explained to the club steward why the Rhodesian Federation would never work; and I wondered if the letter would tell me whether I had passed my Hindustani examination.

I opened the envelope and saw the familiar salutation and valedictory but arguably accurate:

"I have the honour to be,
Your obedient servant"

How often I had signed similarly worded letters. "It is proposed to change the posting arranged for your return to Fiji and, if you agree, to second you as Secretary to the Government of Tonga. It will be necessary for you to cancel your sea passages from the

United Kingdom to New Zealand and to fly to Fiji immediately after the Coronation . . ."

First reactions are usually superficial. I had sweated through Fijian language examinations just before going on leave. Then Hindustani. Now I was to be faced with yet another language. Margaret, a *Hansard* Reporter in the Fiji Legislative Council, had travelled daily from Oxford to London during a bitter winter to take a course in steno-typing for introduction when she returned. We were all set for a relaxing sea voyage. Why should we jettison all this in order to sit out three years of rustication in Tonga?

That night I cabled my acceptance and totted up what little I knew of the eastern neighbour of Fiji.

Tonga was a self-governing British Protected State under a constitutional monarchy with a Privy Council, Cabinet and Legislative Assembly. It was the last Polynesian kingdom, only 400 miles from Fiji to which it was linked by blood, custom and a history of near-successful takeover bids. Captain Cook had called them the Friendly Islands and reputedly left behind a now ancient tortoise. There was a queen called Charlotte named after the consort of George III of England—tall, regal and much loved by her people. And that was about it.

The club library was unrewarding. So, a few days later, were the book shops of Charing Cross Road. At one of these a bespectacled attendant emerged from behind Freud, the Gallic Wars and Molière.

"Have you any books on Fiji or Tonga?" I asked. A pause—no response.

"Have you any books on Fiji or Tonga?"

"Feejee?" You mean the Fijji Islands?"

"Yes," I acquiesced, with the sense of literary fellowship fast disappearing: "I mean the Fijji Islands."

"Ah," regretfully, "no—sorry. What was the other one?"

"Tonga," I said again, with fading hope.

"Who's he? . . . A painter?"

A month later, in June, the Queen of Tonga had endeared herself to a legion of ordinary folk to whom her name and country had meant nothing a few weeks before.

Queen Salote had said goodbye to her people in March. She sailed out of Nuku'alofa on the *Tofua*, the Union Steam Ship Company's modern passenger-cargo ship which comes monthly to unload general freight and take away bananas and other fruit and vegetables for the New Zealand market. The vessel is named after the volcanic island in Tonga on which Captain Bligh landed a party after the *Bounty* mutiny in 1789.

From New Zealand, the Queen set out on her first and what was to be her only journey to Great Britain and Europe. She arrived at Southampton unknown and unheralded. It was not her way to have wished it otherwise. She had frequently slipped in and out of New Zealand and Australia without fuss; and there was, after all, a coronation of world significance with a galaxy of foreign delegations and Commonwealth rulers and representatives.

Nonetheless, Queen Salote commanded interest and speculation from the moment of her arrival in England. She was the only reigning monarch and queen to attend the Coronation; and as the Press liked to describe her, she was the tallest Queen of the smallest Kingdom. Above all, her infectious charm cast a spell over London and wherever she went. I was soon, in Tonga, to discover why.

Like millions of others, we saw her for the first time in the Coronation procession. As the rulers and heads of State moved into the Mall on the return to Buckingham Palace, the swelling cheers seemed to bear down on us like a storm gathering momentum, sweeping all before it.

Then we were one with it, on our feet in the heated excitement of the moment, waving and cheering as Her Tongan Majesty's carriage drove from Westminster Abbey. There she was, the Queen of Tonga, waving a damp handkerchief and mopping her dripping forehead. Withal, her royal smile—a smile that was to light up the corridors of conversation throughout Britain that night and for a long time to come.

Queen Salote was the outstanding overseas figure at the Coronation. Both then and during her subsequent public appearances in England, Northern Ireland and Europe, where she had an audience with the Pope, she left an indelible impression of majestic friendliness. Such was her popularity that songs were composed in her honour, a racehorse was named after her, and June babies were christened Charlotte.

She had, of course, a Tongan way of responding to the warmth of her welcome. *'Ofa* is the Tongan word for love; and *'ofeina* is the love shown to a stranger in another land. When her second daughter-in-law, Princess Melenaite, gave birth to a daughter, the Queen was invited to select a name for her new grandchild. From England, Queen Salote chose 'Ofeina meaning, in this case, the love shown to her by the people of the United Kingdom. In this way, the memory of her visit has been perpetuated in the royal house of Tonga.

The reaction of her people to the popular acclaim accorded to Queen Salote in Britain was understandably more composed than that of the Coronation crowds which greeted her. There was quiet acceptance that London's response to their Queen would be so. How else could it be? Yet there was a thirst for detailed description and eye-witness verification of the fervour of Queen Salote's reception. Tonga had no newspaper or radio and, apart from an official daily news sheet, no public news medium of any kind existed. Many were the tales that were passed on through village and island by word of mouth.

Weeks later, in a village near Nuku'alofa, the talk drifted round to Queen Salote's personal triumph in the Coronation procession and I was asked about her drive through the chill London rain. When I confirmed what had been told them by others, a relative of the Queen who had remained silent during the conversation looked up and spoke.

"Yes, when I heard about our Queen driving in the rain through the streets of London, I knew immediately why Her Majesty had done so."

The speaker paused to engage the attention of his audience.

"In the old days, as you know, the form of public salutation to our chiefs was to drop everything you were carrying and to crouch at the roadside with the head sunk between the knees. Even now, if a high chief passes he should dismount from a horse or bicycle, remove a hat and lower an umbrella. And in this," he said, "we Tongans do not differ greatly from the people of England, Scandinavia and other countries where public respect is still paid, I understand, to those of royal birth. It is our Queen who has taught us love and respect for the customs of our land; and Her Majesty has shown us how she too follows them though she be far from her people."

Much has been written about the circumstances of Queen Salote's historic ride in the rain. Most of it inaccurately reflects the Queen's real reason for her action. It was this. Queen Elizabeth was travelling in a closed coach; accordingly, rain or no rain, the Queen of Tonga declined to have her own carriage covered, in spite of the uncomprehending discomfort of the Malay Sultan travelling with her. Neither the thousands who acclaimed her nor the commentators who warmed to her could have known that her action was an expression of royal Tongan humility in London. To have done otherwise would have infringed the customs of which the Queen was both the repository and the pillar.

One afternoon at Her Majesty's Palace, I remembered the explanation given to me and asked the Queen whether it was correct.

"Yes," she said, "It is. Though I was in London, I still felt and thought as a Tongan; and in our custom I would never cover my carriage in a procession with Her Majesty Queen Elizabeth II, no matter how wet and cold I might be. You see, in the Tongan way, no one may draw attention to himself or make a disturbance in the presence of a person of higher rank. You will understand if I tell you one or two stories to illustrate what I mean.

"When I was about six years old, I accompanied my father, the King, on a journey to Ha'apai and Vava'u. We arrived at Ha'ano in Ha'apai, and on the afternoon when we came to leave it was found that the anchor had been caught under a rock. The men from Ha'ano started diving for the anchor, and an old man called 'Aisea was one of them. 'Aisea was so concerned about this mishap to the King's journey that he continued to search for the elusive anchor and, apparently overcome with exhaustion, he did not reappear. No one knew what had befallen him until his lifeless body floated to the surface.

"I remember, too, a day about a year later when I was returning from the ceremony of the dedication of a new boat. Travelling in the carriage behind me was the grandmother of Tuna 'Ulukalala-'Ata, the wife of the present Minister of Police. As they turned a corner, the third finger of her right hand was caught in the cart-wheel and severed save for a shred of skin. She uttered no cry of pain and I first learned about it when I was told that she had gone for medical attention.

"In 1918 I visited Ha'alaufuli in Vava'u shortly after I had become Queen. We were walking to the village when a swarm of hornets, which I suppose we had disturbed, descended upon one of my attendants. When we arrived I noticed her face was puffed up and I asked her what had happened. She told me she had been attacked by hornets.

" 'Didn't they hurt you?' I asked.

" 'Yes,' she replied, 'but I could not cry out while I was following Your Majesty.'

"Then," continued Queen Salote, "there is a story which has now become almost legendary in our history. In 1852, the town of Pea in Tongatapu was under siege by the warriors of Ha'apai led by King George Tupou I. Inside were people who opposed the adoption of Christianity. Suddenly a spear, hurled from the fort, went through the abdomen of one of the King's men whose name was Liemalohi. The King turned to him and said, 'Lie, you are wounded.' Although in great distress, Lie broke the spear leaving the spearhead inside and replied, 'Your Majesty, it is not words but deeds that count!'

"When the battle had been won, King George asked Lie what he would wish done for him. Lie replied, 'As long as I can see again the white sand of the beach at Ha'apai, I will know that I have reached home, and will die in peace in the knowledge that I have done my duty.'

"So sail was set for Ha'apai; and when Lie was shown the white sand he pulled the spearhead out of his body and surrendered himself to death. He was buried at his village of Koulo where the name Liemalohi is still an appointed title, whose origin is in this story of great bravery in battle."

The Queen smiled gravely and paused. Then that sense of

girlish fun, always bubbling below her regal dignity, burst through.

"There's another little story that I haven't been indiscreet enough to tell anyone yet." Her eyes sparkled as she laughed.

"I was so sorry for the Sultan. He was cold and miserable in the rain and at last he could stand it no longer.

" 'Rain. Cold. Get wet. Close roof?' he asked, as he crouched in his corner of our damp carriage and tried to persuade me to agree to what he wanted.

"I was naughty. 'No understand. No speak English,' I replied and looked as if I did not appreciate what he was talking about.

"At last, the poor Sultan gave in and stayed silent and unhappy for the rest of our journey. I hope that he does not think too ill of me now."

. . . So the Queen of Tonga, whose mastery of elegant English was complete, drove on uncovered through the Coronation rain.

3 Princess and Queen

UNTIL the sixth year of his reign in 1899, King George Tupou II had declined to marry. Overtures had been made to more than one princess, but at length he yielded to pressure from his chiefs and announced his betrothal to ʻOfa, a girl of the second Royal Family, the *Haʻatakalaua*. His Majesty was, however, also attracted to Lavinia Veiongo, in whom he found attributes which ʻOfa seemed not to possess. Lavinia was plainer than the beautiful ʻOfa; but whereas ʻOfa was proud and aloof, Lavinia was demure and humble. At the last moment, the King changed his mind and decided to marry Lavinia and not ʻOfa. When the nobles met to remonstrate with him, His Majesty announced that if he were not to marry the girl of his choice, he would not marry at all. The party who supported the King trotted out the relevant section of the Constitution. They pointed out that inasmuch as "it shall not be lawful for any member of the Royal Family likely to succeed to the throne, to marry any person without the consent of the King", the King himself was obviously free to give his consent to his own marriage with any person he pleased.

The nobles were disconcerted and the meeting dispersed in confusion. Public opinion was divided and the country was torn by factious rift. For a time, the nobles broke off relations with their sovereign and made no effort to discover the perpetrators of the outrages which then began. There were attempts to set fire to public buildings and the houses of unpopular members of the Royal Family. Undismayed, the King proceeded to marry Lavinia and it was their daughter, Salote Mafileʻo Pilolevu, who succeeded him as Queen on the 5th April, 1918, three weeks after her eighteenth birthday.

The year 1900 is of special significance in Tonga. On the 2nd May, the King had signed an agreement about his relations with foreign powers so that his affairs might be conducted under the sole advice of the British Government and that "Her Britannic Majesty shall protect His Majesty's dominions from external hostile attacks". After long and delicate negotiations between the King and Basil Thomson, the British Envoy Extraordinary, Tonga became a British Protected State. Although its terms have been changed with the passing of time, the basis of that agreement remains today.

Seven weeks before, on the 13th March, Princess Salote had been born to Queen Lavinia at the Palace in Nuku'alofa; and when he visited Tonga in May, the Prime Minister of New Zealand, the Right Honourable Richard John Seddon, provided this description of the royal child:

> An adjournment to the Palace was then made, a wish having been expressed that the likeness of the baby prince [*sic*] should be taken by the photographer of the expedition who had gone to the Palace with that expectation; but he was kept standing on the grass under the watchful eye of the armed sentry who evidently distrusted the appearance of the artist and doubted the innocence of the box containing the camera. We were admitted to the throne room and were received by Her Majesty the Queen of Tonga. The Queen is a graceful and elegant young woman and bore herself during the trying interview with many strangers in a manner that evoked admiration. She was admirably robed in a dark silk dress of the latest European fashion and wore the costume as "to the manner born".
>
> The King did not appear and would not bear the child to be taken into the open air to be photographed. The afternoon's sun was getting low and the interior of the room was too dark to allow the portraits to be taken inside the house. It appeared that the infant had not yet been christened and that some point of court etiquette would be infringed if the child was to leave the Palace before the ceremony had been gone through. The baby, however, was brought down to the room in which we were, and was duly admired and kissed by the lady visitors. It was a good baby and behaved with great serenity and decorum, never crying when the strange white faces crowded around it . . .

The same serenity and decorum, apparent to one observer at such an early age, was to be the distinction of Queen Salote's personality and character throughout her life. It was true that the baby could not leave the Palace before the day of christening which is normally performed three months after birth. Until that time, a Tongan child does not go outside the house of the parents. To do otherwise in the case of a royal child was unthinkable.

The baby Princess was only two years old when her mother died on the 25th April, 1902; and later, the young Princess loved to hear stories of the mother she had never really known. In 1909, at the age of nine, she left Tonga for Auckland where she was enrolled at the Church of England Diocesan School for Girls. She returned to Tonga to marry Prince Uiliami Tupoulahi Tungi on the 19th September, 1917. At 18, the new Queen was a slender handsome girl with the captivating smile which never left her. She was proclaimed Queen of Tonga a few hours after her father's death on the 5th April, 1918. After six months of court and national mourning, a proclamation was issued notifying her installation as Tu'i Kanokupolu in the royal *kava* ring. The ceremony was held in the Palace grounds with the dignity and solemnity of historic procedure. The Queen sat on a decorated dais under an elaborate canopy of palms and garlands of chiefly flowers. Offerings of food were made from all parts of the kingdom. A huge *kava* root was presented to the Queen and the *kava* was then prepared in the traditional manner. When the *kava* had been drunk and the presentations of food distributed to the nobles and the lesser chiefs forming the *kava* circle, there were speeches recognising the right of the girl queen to the throne of Tonga. Two days later, on the 11th October, 1918, Salote was crowned Queen of Tonga in the Royal Chapel.

The links with Britain were personal as well as dynastic. Queen Salote was the third sovereign of the line of Tupou, founded by her great great grandfather, King George Tupou I, in 1845. King George and his Queen embraced Christianity in 1831. At their baptisms they had assumed the names of Jioji (George) and Salote (Charlotte), in honour of King George III of England and his consort, Queen Charlotte.

As a girl, Salote loved music and frequently played the piano at the Palace. She inherited this love from her father and has handed it on to her two sons. She was a composer of many Tongan songs of love and lament. Often, the reply to the questioner who asked the name of the composer of a lilting melody was "Her Majesty the Queen". She never took part publicly in Tongan dances; but she frequently composed the music and words for their performance. Unlike Samoa, where men and women of chiefly birth join in their dances of rejoicing, women of the Tongan Royal Family do not do so. It is rare for a man or woman of chiefly birth to dance in public.

The first Christian missionaries reached the Friendly Islands in 1797, when ten artisans came "in the capacity of missionaries". After a period of ill-treatment and failure, the mission was abandoned and they left for New South Wales. In 1822, Walter Lawry of the Wesleyan Missionary Society arrived. He subsequently described the Tongan view of missionaries as "harbingers of soldiers who would shortly come to kill them and seize their land". He was not surprised that "they consequently treated me with suspicion". Other missionaries followed and with the acceptance of Christianity by King George Tupou I, Tonga set out, under the guiding hand of its Wesleyan clerics, on the road to *sivilaise* or "civilisation".

It was perhaps in search of this elusive quality that the Tongan Royal house and nobles came to desert their traditional dress and adopted the stiff-necked attire of Victorian England. The early photographs show them in starched butterfly collars, waistcoats, close-fitting black jackets and striped trousers. On state occasions, a black top hat was perched on a perspiring noble brow. The young Queen began to reflect about the artificially transplanted vestments of European royalty. She saw that they could bring about a loss of her people's sense of identity. Not surprisingly, there was opposition to forsaking these signs of progress. So it was not until after the second world war, her husband having died in 1941, that Queen Salote achieved the return of Tongan dress on public occasions. The fashion of wearing alien clothes gradually died out; and dignity and grace was restored to the court of Tonga.

The origin of this change lay in the Queen's desire to preserve the customs of her people against the impact of an impatient world which, she foresaw, was going to press heavily on the social structure of her country. She well knew what would happen to her people if knowledge of their traditions were to be lost: the unity of Tonga would be in jeopardy. As she once remarked: "There is a generation of young people growing up now who do not know who they are and to whom they belong. If Tonga is to survive, the ties of kinship must be strengthened, not loosened."

Her detailed knowledge of her subjects and their kinship groups was remarkable. She knew and could elucidate the family tree and intricate relationships of her nobles and lesser chiefs. She could name fathers, mothers, cousins and offspring of numerous others. Her decision was constantly sought in respect of land ownership and boundary disputes. The Queen was concerned that her personal knowledge should not be lost and, in 1955, she set up a Traditions Committee, the object of which was to record custom and genealogy for posterity. She feared that when she died her store of knowledge would die with her unless it were written down by those of her people who shared her recognition of its value to the survival of the Tongan way of life.

As Chairman of the Committee, Queen Salote appointed Ve'ehala, Keeper of the Palace Records, one of the Nobles and her close confidant. Already known for his own deep interest in history and custom, Ve'ehala was a genial man of irresistible versatility. The reigning Nureyev of Tongan dancing and maestro of the nose flute, he was a rotund Polynesian Friar Tuck. His laugh was a rich asset at any social occasion and his linguistic skill was notable. He and I had shared the same Latin master at Auckland Grammar School; and he was equally at home in Tongan, English, Fijian and Samoan. He now compères a weekly listeners' request session from the Tonga Broadcasting Commission radio station in Nuku'alofa. This is beamed to Samoa, Fiji and New Zealand as well as Tonga; and Ve'ehala's announcements are made in the richly rounded phrases of any of four languages in the one programme. He it was who first revealed to me the clarity with which descent can be traced in Tonga: "Holonga is the

Queen Salote waving to the cheering London crowds at the Coronation

Queen Salote with her grandson Prince Taufa'ahau, now the Crown Prince

place where Queen Lavinia's paternal grandfather's mother's descendants now live. In the old days it was attached to Vuna Tu'i-Vava'u and the Ha'a Havea tribe. Ika Manu'uli was one of the Ha'a Havea petty chiefs and his daughter Finau Holonga had a daughter Temaleti; Temaleti's son was 'Inoke Fotu; his son was Kupu-a-vanua, who was Queen Lavinia's father; and Queen Lavinia was Queen Salote's mother."

History and custom have been perpetuated in the names chosen by the Queen for her grandchildren and for ships and houses. Her youngest grandchild is 'Ahoeitu. Queen Salote named him after the first Tu'i Tonga.

The name is a thousand years old and would not be assumed by an ordinary Tongan family. The Government ship *Hifofua* bears the name of a tournament of the Tu'i Kanokupolu.

The Queen's residence in Auckland was named 'Atalanga to commemorate the legendary fisherman. A second house nearby, bought in 1955 as a hostel for Tongan students, was named Va'epopua by Queen Salote. Va'epopua was the name of the mother of the first Tu'i Tonga. She can therefore be said to be the maternal chiefly progenitor of the Tongan people.

There are outward signs by which the Tongan acknowledges relationships. Margaret has a Tongan name—Anga'ae-fonu—which means "the sadness that comes from the tears of the turtle". Fonu—the turtle—for short. She was born in Fiji and was aware, when we went to Tonga, that her family was distantly connected with the Royal family; but Tongan custom is such that a person of lower rank does not claim or proclaim such a relationship. To do so, would be *laupisi*—boastful and pretentious. The Tongan, the Royal family not excluded, nonetheless expresses the warmth of his relationship. The most common practice is for the high-ranking member of the family to acknowledge kinship by kissing the lesser member of the clan on the cheek, when they meet. Men and women both do this, in private or in public.

It was on the birth of our first daughter in Nuku'alofa that the recognition of family became a touching experience. On the morning after the baby's birth, Princess Mata'aho and Princess Melenaite arrived at the hospital with special gift mats and *tapa* to express pleasure at our good fortune. Mata'aho also brought with her the name which the Queen had graciously chosen to give to the new child. This was 'Atu-o-hakautapu, a name taken from the Queen's own family line. It meant "the bonito fish from the sacred reef"; and we call her 'Atu for short. Later, the Queen asked to be informed of the christening day as she wanted to be present. When it came, Her Majesty watched the ceremony in the great new Wesleyan Church in Nuku'alofa with a closeness and unconcealed warmth of affection.

With the christening over, Margaret, observing a Tongan custom, took the new babe to the Palace to be presented to the Queen. With her was the baby's christening cake for Her Majesty. Genial Bella Riechelmann, who managed the solitary boarding house in Nuku'alofa, had made and iced a celebration cake which was indeed fit for a Queen. An air of family dispensation of protocol seemed to pervade the Palace. Unannounced, Margaret arrived with the baby after the church service and informed one of the Queen's attendants that she had come to show Her Majesty the newly christened child. A message was taken upstairs. Shortly after, the Queen appeared on the stairway. Margaret describes her on that occasion as a resplendent figure, her most gracious, her most charming. She was dressed in a purple dress with a ruffled collar and long sleeves looking like a picture-book Queen—the young Victoria perhaps. Young at heart was always the impression she created even though, on this occasion, her silver white hair was such a crowning contrast with the purple of her dress which was ankle length and demurely covered the full length of her arms.

"I was just writing 'Atu's family tree for you. Here it is. It goes back ten generations and the name hasn't been used since then." Queen Salote was warm and generous as she gazed at the brown-eyed baby. Later that day, as we celebrated the christening of our first child with a feast in Tongan style, gifts of food—yams and a pig—arrived from the Palace.

Queen Salote's compassion for the young was also expressed through her sensitive understanding of the teenager. Margaret had worked at the British Consulate for a time before 'Atu was born. She became intrigued by the apparent frustrations of young extrovert Tongans who appeared on the steps of the Consulate with petitions to the United Nations and the Secretary of State for the Colonies. Bearded and sullen, they preached against authority in the streets. They attracted little attention—the *haua*, or loafers, they were called. But they presented a problem and they had a case to argue. Basically, they were bored, unstimulated, resentful. They seemed to be getting nowhere. Margaret thought that what the young men longed for most was for someone to take some notice of them. So, after a number of petitions had been presented at the Consulate, she asked the leader of the group if they would like to make use of a small wooden building in our grounds at Fongoloa to use as they wished, to read, sing and play games. In this way, we got to know them—Sunipa, Christiani, Viliami and many others. They sometimes came into the house to sit on the floor with us and sing and talk. Soon their street-corner orations became less frequent and the flow of petitions came to an end.

The Queen heard about the conversion of these renegades of her capital. After a time we received a message that Her Majesty would be happy to have "Fonu's boys", as she called them, perform an item in an annual concert which the Queen sponsored. Her Majesty did not attend the public performance, but it was a Royal Command Performance in the true sense, since she selected the performers, undertook the role of royal producer, and viewed the dress rehearsal to see that it was up to standard.

Queen Salote chuckled with girlish amusement when she saw "Fonu's boys", the town loafers, acting a mock court, the real-life procedure for which was fully familiar to them. Typically, the boys told us nothing of their reaction to this royal invitation. It was sufficient that the Queen watched them from the wings with a lively and critical eye.

There were times when Queen Salote gave a pointed lesson in correct customary procedure in return for generous but mistaken tribute to her. Should gifts of food, mats or *tapa* arrive at the Palace for presentation on the occasion of a wedding or death, she might ask, "Who is this from?" If the gift had not come to her in the right way it might be politely sent back. The Queen would ask that it be presented first to the local chief who would then pass on that portion of it which by custom went to the sovereign.

It is tempting to be sentimental about Queen Salote in retrospect. It was impossible not to feel the same about her during her lifetime. There were some who came to Nuku'alofa doubting whether they would find the sovereign who had enraptured London. Afterwards, their reaction was the same. Heads of state, admirals, politicians, generals, emerged from the throne room at the Palace in admiration of the Queen of Tonga. There was never a hint of condescension in her regal splendour on formal occasions. Perhaps this was the reason. But matching it, was a disarming girlish charm. They were rare complementary attributes.

Whether she spoke in English or Tongan, her voice had a compelling warmth and softness, which was unassuming yet unmistakably authoritative. To hear her speak without seeing her, made it hard to believe that English was her second language; and limpid dignity of style was the hallmark of her personal writings.

The Queen's compassion for her people was derived in large measure from her deep Christian conviction. As Head of the State Church she was always present, until she became too ill to go, in the special place reserved for the Royal Family in the great Wesleyan Church of Nuku'alofa. In 1964, some 300 women from thirteen countries came to Tonga at the Queen's invitation to attend a meeting of the Pan Pacific South East Asia Women's Association. There were no hotels and only one small boarding house in Nuku'alofa. Because of their love of their Queen, many families opened their simple homes to the visitors.

It was her last international occasion. She was already suffering from the early ravages of her illness.

4 Polynesian Political Initiation

THE day after my arrival in Nuku'alofa, the Tongan Legislative Assembly was in session. To my surprise, I found myself the subject of a debate which occupied the members for nearly two days.

The legislators of the Friendly Islands are twenty-two in number and they believe in making the most of their deliberations. The primary purpose of their annual gathering in Nuku'alofa was to examine with praiseworthy thoroughness, the government estimates of revenue and expenditure presented for their consideration by a Treasurer and Minister of Finance who had been patiently holding the purse strings of the Kingdom since 1949. Originally from New Zealand he had served the interests of the Tongan people since 1927. The Kingdom had no national debt and those of the Treasurer's financial critics who observed that, in consequence, it had little development, did not get much of a hearing. The Ministers of the Crown were proud of their solvency. National indebtedness came close to jeopardising national independence. This no responsible Tongan could abide.

Now, as is well known, Parliamentary Keepers of the Public Purse are targets of professional and amateur polemics wherever the black budget box exists. Tonga is no exception. There were emotionally charged pleas that all the money set out in the estimates should be available in cash for inspection by Honourable Members —preferably in the House itself—before expenditure was approved. At the very least, a Representative of the People should be permitted to ensure that whatever was left over from the previous year was produced for all to see. There was no suggestion of casting a slur on the financial integrity of the Minister of Finance but as a parliamentarian, one was entitled to certain considerations and the People expected to be told the truth. After all, if the money was there, it would only take the Minister a few minutes to bring it over from the Treasury.

On one occasion, the Treasurer, in a fit of pique, told a persistently irritating questioner that the cash reserves of the Kingdom were in the safe in his office. And where did he expect them to be anyway—in the lavatory? This provoked the assembled legislators who rose in protest. The Tongan equivalent of "withdraw" echoed round the Chamber until the Treasurer, sensing disapproval even among his Ministerial colleagues, succumbed to pressure and did withdraw.

On another day, the House was in committee and in earnest debate on the emoluments of the staff of the Governor of Vava'u, as proposed in a salaries revision report.

Tu'akoi, Representative of the People of Tongatapu, lawyer, ex-policeman and tireless talker on every conceivable subject, catches the eye of the Chairman and rises to ask the Minister of Finance a question.

The Minister of Finance also rises, as is the custom, and gazes across the floor of the House as he wonders what is coming now.

"*Minisita Pa'anga,*" asks Tu'akoi guilelessly "how much do you spend on food each month?"

The Minister of Finance grasps the table in front of him, pauses and confesses that he does not know.

"Would it," continues his questioner, "be more than £20 a month?"

The Treasurer considers his state of personal penury and sees the possibility of parliamentary support for an improvement.

"Much more," he says emphatically, "very much more than £20."

"Then if that is the case, why is it that the Government contemplates giving the poor hardworked crew of the Governor's launch a ration allowance of only £3 per month?"

Not having a ready answer for this, the Treasurer murmurs that that is different. He isn't really sure why, so he does not enlarge on this brief reply. Both Lords and Commons reflect sagely that perhaps there is something in what Tu'akoi says.

Now it was unfortunate, in a sense, that all this should have to be

Tonga. **Fika 5 ‘oe 1955.**

‘Oku ou loto ki ai.

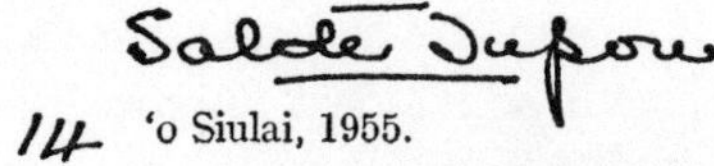

14 ‘o Siulai, 1955.

KOE LAO

KE FAKAHU ATU ‘AE PA‘ANGA KI HE NGAHI NGAUE ‘OE PULE‘ANGA.

[1 ‘o Siulai, 1955]

‘OKU TU‘UTU‘UNI ‘e he Tu‘i moe Fale Alea ‘o Tonga ‘i he Fakataha Alea ‘oe Pule‘anga ‘o pehe :—

1. Koe hingoa nounou ‘oe Lao ni Koe Lao ke Fakahu atu ‘ae Pa‘anga 1955-56 ki he ngahi Ngaue ‘oe Pule‘anga 1955, pea ‘e lau ne kamata ngaue‘aki kamata mei he ‘aho ‘uluaki ‘o Siulai, 1955. HINGOA NOUNOU.

2. ‘E fakahu mo ngaue ‘aki ki he ngaue ‘oe Pule‘anga ‘i he ta‘u ‘oku ngata ‘i he ‘aho tolungofulu ‘o Sune taha afe hivangeau nimangofulu ma ono ‘ae pa‘anga ‘o ‘ikai lahi hake ‘i he sovaleni ‘e nima kilu nima mano ono afe nimangeau ma fitu ke totongi ‘aki ‘ae ngahi ngaue ‘oe Pule‘anga ‘o Tonga ‘i he ta‘u koia. Pea ‘e vahevahe ‘o hange ko‘eni :— £556,507 KE TOTONGI ‘AE NGAHI NGAUE ‘OE PULE‘ANGA KI HE 1955-56.

	£
I.—Ko ‘Ene ‘Afio koe Tu‘i	12,000
II.—Fale Alea	5,991
III.—Palemia	19,015
IVa.—Kovana, Ha‘apai	2,561
IVb.—Kovana, Vava‘u	2,431
V.—‘Aotita	3,814
VI.—Fale Pa‘anga	10,663
VII.—Fale Tute moe Positi ‘Ofisi	13,631
VIII.—Fonua moe Fua Fonua	13,520

The first page of an Act passed by the Legislative Assembly and signed by Queen Salote

spoken in the Tongan language since it was directed to the one man in the House who could not understand what was being said. In spite of his years in Tonga, the Treasurer spoke no Tongan. Happily, however, he had an interpreter whose duty it was to absorb the flow of Tongan oratory in the House and, at the same time, to reproduce it discreetly into the ear of one cut off from his colleagues by that most humbling of barriers—language.

The reverse process was, of course, neither so quiet nor so discreet. The interpretation from English to Tongan had to be audible to all; and while the interpreter might have felt impelled on occasion to water down the disputatiousness of his fellow Tongans, he had no such tactful compunction when interpreting back into his own tongue. The Treasurer, ignorant of how things were going, often did not wait for the interpreter to finish. The House then had them both going full bore, since nothing makes a man raise his voice more than when he thinks he is not being properly understood.

The Government estimates were made out under the usual heads and subheads. They were considered in detail by a committee of the whole House. The Parliamentary expenditure, immediately following the Queen's Privy Purse and including the daily allowances paid to the members in attendance, was passed with commendable rapidity within a day or two of the opening of the session. Unfortunately, this did not apply to the rest of the proposed public expenditure about which lengthy and often tendentious discussion went on for about six or eight weeks. This would not have mattered so much had the Legislative Assembly not begun its examination of the new year's estimates only about a week or so before the end of the old; and there was no provision for interim expenditure in the early part of the new financial year. As a result, houses were being repaired, patients were being treated with drugs, and civil servants paid from money which had not yet been voted.

Sometimes individual Members took a dislike to a particular civil servant or project and, as like as not, attempted to disapprove the funds for his salary or the scheme concerned, irrespective of the consequences. All this was blissfully unknown to me as the

Legislative Assembly began to tackle the Premier's Office estimates, and my own post and salary came under fire in the Committee of Supply.

Tu'akoi: Mr. Chairman, can I ask the Premier a question? Why is the Government Secretary being paid more than the Premier?

Acting Premier: The Secretary's salary is not paid according to our local salary scales, but in accordance with the terms of his agreement.

Tu'akoi: I had no idea that any Secretary's salary would be higher than the Premier's.

Treasurer: Mr. Chairman, can I explain this matter to the Member? I wish you would read the notes properly. How do you make out that the Secretary receives a higher salary than the Premier?

Tu'akoi: Is not £1,700 more than £1,100?

Treasurer: No. Possibly, at the end of three years the Secretary's salary will reach £920. I think that he is probably on £840 now. The salary scales mentioned in the Estimates are the scales in which they are being paid.

Tu'akoi: How much does the present Secretary get?

Treasurer: I think £840, Fiji currency.

Tu'akoi: Mr. Chairman, I think that it is only right that we should reduce the Secretary's salary. It is not appropriate for any member of a staff to receive more than his head. If he stays here long enough he will get more than the Premier. Another thing, there is an Assistant Secretary at £520 and a new officer at £645 as well as a Relieving Officer at £583: how many Europeans are you going to have in this office? Why not pay the Tongan boys more and let them do the work? The Assistant Secretary was late to work this morning: he did not come until 9 o'clock, and in the meantime the Tongan boys who are on a much lower salary have to carry on the office work. What work do the two

Secretaries do? What will the two Relieving Officers do? I move that Item 5, Relieving Officer, be expunged from the Estimates.

Finau: I support the motion. The Premier and the Treasurer should explain the reason for this large increase from £1,200 to £2,000, an increase of £800. The old Secretary is being paid £1,053 plus £211 as pension contribution, making a total of £1,200; while the new Secretary will start on £1,700 plus £330 as pension contribution making a total of £2,000. I would support that the new Secretary be paid the same salary as the retiring Secretary. The House should be informed why the salary is increased from £1,200 to £2,000. It should be carefully considered that if we cannot get an appointee to this post then just leave it. What correspondence is of such importance that the Premier cannot dictate to the typist? Why should we spend all this money? I see no reason at all for spending this £2,000; just pay the new Secretary what the retiring Secretary was getting. If not then just let the Assistant Secretary do the work.

Acting Premier: The Government does not recruit officers indiscriminately. The post of Secretary is one of the most responsible posts in the Service. One member has mentioned that the Premier be his own secretary. All I can say to that is that I hope that we shall never come to that stage. The Premier and the Secretary have their own respective duties to perform. These Estimates have been very carefully considered, and it was decided that these posts are essential to the smooth running of the Government. By this motion, the Government is being blamed for recruiting officers who can be dispensed with. Let me assure the House that there is no such thing. No Tongan can fill the post of Secretary and certain Members may say that the job is an easy one. Anyone can stand up in this House and say that the job is easy, but when it comes to doing it, that is a different story. You have power to reduce or cancel the post altogether, but I hope it will never come to that.

Finau: The Premier has failed to give the House the reason for this increase from £1,200 to £2,000. I especially requested him for an explanation. We are not as dumb as he thinks. Every time a European replacement takes place that new officer comes on a higher salary. So I would move that the post be abolished.

Afuha'amango: I would like to support the motion from this table that the post of Secretary be abolished. The Acting Premier may be right in what he said, but he must remember that we have been in this world much longer than he has, and he does not know a thing. We really want to know why there are so many Europeans in the service. You have talked about the Secretary. Just let me be Secretary. How many times have I asked the House to test all the Government servants and let all the posts that can be filled by Tongans be filled by Tongans. Only appoint Europeans to posts that cannot be filled by Tongans. We will probably pay this new man £8 a day. Why not let Her Majesty and Her Ministers run the Kingdom themselves. As it is now, the Ministers have no power at all, all they do is to say please, sorry. Why should these Europeans be paid such high salaries? Gandhi asked for self-government in India, because the Indians themselves could run the Government themselves. India is now enjoying herself. If you disagree, then you had better retire from the post and let us run the Government. Let us run our own Government and country. Nothing on earth is difficult, getting to heaven is the only thing that is difficult. So let us abolish the post of Secretary.

Minister of Works: As mentioned by the Acting Premier, if the Government could dispense with the services of the Secretary it would have done so. We all know the various duties performed by the Secretary. Besides the office work, he is also a member of the Staff Board, Copra Board,

Banana Board, Electric Light Board. Everything that goes through Cabinet and Privy Council must be handled by him. Be not angry and wish to have the post abolished, for it is a very responsible post, and no Tongan can fill it. If we abolish the post of Secretary we will be like a boat without a steersman, so I would move that the Premier's Estimates be passed.

S. A. Kaho: I have been a member of this House since 1919 and I have never struck this before. No replacement was ever paid higher than the officer he was replacing. So I am quite surprised at the new Secretary being paid a higher salary than the retiring Secretary. Now this Secretary will be paid more than the Premier. Where is he from?

Acting Premier: This officer is being seconded from Fiji on the same salary as he was getting in Fiji, and should we reduce his salary he will return to Fiji by the next boat.

At this point the debate ended for the day. The Representatives of the People resumed the attack on the following morning.

Tu'akoi: According to page 8 of the Estimates, the Secretary's salary is £1,700 for 1953/54, but on the notes on page 8 his salary goes up to £1,300. Why the difference?

Treasurer: Mr. Chairman, I tried to explain this matter yesterday, but evidently I did not succeed. At the moment we have two Secretaries here, Mr. Lake and Mr. Bain. Mr. Lake will be leaving Tonga quite shortly and his salary is about £F840, whilst Mr. Bain's salary is very much the same. Mr. Lake will be granted vacation leave and during that time he will be receiving his salary from the Tonga Government. So for a while we will be paying two Secretaries' salaries, and the £1,700 will pay the two salaries. The new Secretary's salary of £840 will start from the day he left Fiji, which was the 30th June, I think.

Tu'akoi: Why does not he start off at £600 as shown on the notes?

Treasurer: The notes only give you the salary scale within which he will be paid. He has already had about nine years service. The Government considers this post to be a very responsible one and it ought to be filled by a member of the Colonial Service.

Tu'akoi: Which is the more responsible post, the Treasurer or the Secretary?

Treasurer: The Treasurer.

Acting Premier: I wish to thank the Honourable Members for all they have said. I am sure that they all wish to do their best for Tonga. It is apparent that the aim of the Representatives of the People is to persuade the House that the time has come for Tongans to run the Government themselves. I and all the Ministers maintain that it is still impossible. We must still have the assistance of European officers. Mention has been made of these Tongan boys who have had education overseas. Let me assure the House that not one of them can fill the post of Secretary. The job of Secretary requires special training. I would say once again that these boys have not the necessary qualifications to fill the post. Although these boys may be able to speak and write English quite fluently, the job of Secretary requires far more than that. Not only that but a Secretary must have a good knowledge of our international relationships with other nations with whom we have dealings. I know that you are taking this attitude for patriotic reasons, but I love my country just as much as you do. So the only way you can show your love is to get the officer who will render the best service for your country. The new Secretary is a man from Great Britain and is a member of the Colonial Service, and should we decide to lower his salary today, I assure you that he will leave by the next boat, and it will be very very difficult to get another man to fill his place. What will happen to our relationship with Great Britain if we should turn round and send this Secretary back? Let us consider the future. Will Britain be willing to send more officers to Tonga if that is the way we treat these officers it has picked for Tonga? So Mr. Chairman, let us consider this question from all angles, before we do anything that we might be sorry for later. What will Her Majesty think when she hears that the Government has refused to have this officer, whom the Colonial Office has so kindly seconded to us. It is my belief, Mr. Chairman, that the time will come when Tonga will be self-contained, but at the present time we are still without suitable men, and consequently we are still dependent on England for our officers. The salary is by no means very high, for the difference between the two salaries is only about £40. Let me tell you again that none of you can do the job. These Secretaries are University men, but none of the boys mentioned have been to the University.

Mafua: The post is a responsible post, and the holder must be paid a salary worthy of the post, but our financial position must not be forgotten. If the British Government has University men as Secretaries, there is no reason why the Tonga Government should follow suit.

Finau: It has been pointed out to us that this amount of £1,700 represents the salaries of both Secretaries. Can anyone tell me whether the Secretary works better than Tungi (the Premier)? Is he cleverer than Tungi? All the Secretary does is to write two or three letters for the mail. Why can't Tungi dictate it in English to the Assistant Secretary and then have it typed? I am afraid we Tongans have one incurable ailment, that is, we are too fond of saying 'yes' to everything. I would therefore ask the House to abolish the post of Secretary. Nothing will happen if we do not have a Secretary. If we do not abolish the post then let us pay the same salary as we paid the previous Secretary.

Afuha'amango: I have been listening to this debate since yesterday and it is clear to me that the Ministers are just trying to mislead the House. I mentioned yesterday how old I am, so I would like to say now . . .

Acting Premier: Mr. Chairman, the Honourable Member has strayed from the subject under consideration.

Afuha'amango: I have not strayed from the point at all. You mentioned something about the Treaty of Friendship with Great Britain. Can you inform the House of any gift from Britain to Tonga since 1900? There has been none at all. We have no power at all under the Agreement. Great Britain is too clever to commit herself to doing something for which she would be criticised. All you Ministers should say that you cannot do your work, then we will step in and take your jobs, for we are quite capable of doing it. Then you turn round and say that you want University men in the service. We are here to represent the voice of 50,000 people. So I would support the motion that this post be abolished and just tell this man to go back to Fiji.

The Speaker: I would just like to say what I think about the matter under discussion. I am not in favour of abolishing this post. This post is of great importance not only to the Premier but to the Government as well, and you all know the responsibilities of this post. I might agree to the abolition of another post, but I definitely would not agree to abolishing the Secretary. It has been said in the House that Tongans can fill this post, let me tell you that no Tongan can do the job, not even the Ministers. So I still maintain that the time has not yet come when we Tongans can fill this post. So I think that we are quite clear on this question and let us take a vote on it.

Acting Premier: Mr. Chairman, will you please let us take a vote on the subject, for members are just repeating themselves.

Tu'akoi: The motion to abolish the post of Secretary has not been seconded, but the motion to reduce the £1,700 to £1,053 has been supported.

Treasurer: If the estimate is reduced from £1,700 to £1,053, it amounts to abolishing the post. Once the House decides to reduce this money, there will not be sufficient money to pay for the Secretary, and he will be forced to return home.

Tu'akihekolo: Can I ask the Treasurer to split this £1,700 up and inform the House how much each Secretary will get out of it?

Treasurer: I have already explained four times that this £1,700 is the salary of two Secretaries.

Tu'akihekolo: If the Treasurer is not willing to give the two separate salaries, then I am afraid I shall have to support the views expressed by our table.

Treasurer: If you do not trust the Treasurer to prepare these Estimates in the way he thinks best, then you should not have him as Treasurer.

Tu'akihekolo: As the Estimates now stand, Members of the House think that it is the salary of one man only.

Treasurer: Mr. Chairman, I shall want a little time to calculate the two salaries.

Mafua: I would request that the House be adjourned until the Treasurer works out the two salaries.

Acting Premier: I move that we should take a vote on it now, for the Members simply do not want to listen to facts.

Tu'akoi: What shall we vote on?

Acting Premier: That the whole Premier's Estimates be passed.

Tu'akoi: Mr. Chairman, it was first moved and seconded that the Secretary's salary be reduced, and secondly that Item 5 be abolished.

Chairman: Those in favour that the Secretary's salary be reduced, please signify.

Clerk: Seven Members voted for it.

Finau: We should have voted on the last motion first. The last motion was made by the Speaker of the House that the post of new Relieving Clerk be abolished.

The Speaker: That was not my motion, I was only seconding the motion made by the No. 2 Member.

Queen Salote with her royal guests outside the Palace in 1953. Tuimalila, the ancient tortoise, shares the photograph

Queen Salote leaves a feast with her former ADC, Vaea, in 1956

Queen Salote signs a new Treaty of Friendship with Britain in 1957

Chairman: We will vote again. Those in favour that the salary of the Secretary be reduced, please signify.

Clerk: 8 for, 12 against.

Chairman: Those in favour that the Premier's office Estimates be passed please signify.

Clerk: 14 for, 6 against.

At the time, it was like an unexpectedly cold shower. The excitements of the Coronation and the smile of Queen Salote seemed a long way from this; but I didn't yet know of the many faces of Tonga.

For the next three years, the debates went on during the eight-week annual session of the Legislative Assembly with scarcely a ripple of consequence reaching the gentle serenity of life outside. Some of the Members, life-long practitioners of off-beat criticism, hinted and intrigued remorselessly. They debated to an empty public gallery; while outside, in the sunshine, the palm leaves rustled, the coconuts fell and the villager went about his affairs—largely ignorant of it all and caring less, so long as he was left in peace and reasonable comfort.

The day after the debate finished, I saw another aspect of the Tongan panorama, now beginning to unfold. I had brought a new car from England. Atwell, due on leave some days after my arrival, persuaded me that his Morris Minor was more suitable for the narrow roads of Tongatapu. The sale depended on his finding a buyer for my Austin. This he rapidly did. The next afternoon, a young Tongan in aged trousers and shirt was ushered into my office. The sum of £895 in Tongan currency did not, he assured me through the medium of an interpreter, present any insurmountable barrier. He would be along in the morning to clinch the deal. With previous experience of such promises, I thought I would believe him when my bank statement said so.

Next morning he did turn up. I went out to hand the car over to him. He would pay up in a moment, he said—when his mother arrived. Odd, I thought, but perhaps her blessing was essential. Shortly afterwards we were joined by an elderly woman who had alighted from a country bus. She carried a plaited Tongan basket over which was draped a tattered piece of brown paper. With a smile, she handed it to me. What was this—bananas, oranges, a live chicken perhaps? Who knew what the customary formality might be for car sales in Tonga?

I thanked her and took the basket. Beneath the brown paper lay a haphazard pile of £1 Government of Tonga Treasury notes.

"You had better count them to make sure they are all there," suggested my interpreter with admirable good sense.

We did so on the bonnet of the car in the main street of Nuku-'alofa with scarcely a glance from those who passed by. In exchange for precisely 895 £1 notes, I handed over the keys of the car. We shook hands and he went off after an agonised protest from the gearbox.

It was not until I had safely deposited the notes in the capacious hands of the teller at the Government Savings Bank that I could breathe freely again.

When I was handed my salary in cash at the end of the month, I was not quite so taken aback. The weaning process had begun.

5 The Staff of Life Official

APART from an Assistant Secretary from New Zealand, my office staff was Tongan—and an interesting blend of personality, ability and type it was. Saia Vaea was the senior clerk. A dour restless-eyed bachelor of middle age, he lurked behind an all-concealing desk from which he surveyed the proceedings of the clerical day. He was indulged by the Ministers and chiefs partly because of his versatile employ of the honorifics of formal address towards them, and partly because a lengthy association with the Cabinet and Legislative Assembly had made him of value in the matter of record keeping. Chiefly tolerance extended to his assumption of the name Vaea, a title of nobility to which he had debatable customary right. He was a necessary link in the bureaucratic chain.

In his otherwise uncorrupt life, he was guilty of one peccadillo. His principal extra-curricular activity was patronage of the weekly listeners' request session from the Rotorua radio station in New Zealand. Records were often played for listeners in Tonga where evening reception was good for most of the year. The management was at first surprised and then gratified at sustained response from across the Pacific: they might have been even more surprised and not quite so gratified had they known that many of the Nuku'alofa requests came from one man. The "coconut wireless" had it that my chief clerk spent much of his spare time concocting letters each requesting a different record and each signed in a different name. So every week Saia listened to a programme of pop music part of which was of his own choosing.

Across the room from the senior clerk sat the official interpreter, a man of no mean skill in his chosen field and of talent and resource in others. 'Uliti Palu, whom I came to know best of the office staff, was of humble origin; but his linguistic achievements brought him in touch with the highest in the land. He had been educated at

Newington College, Sydney, and had returned to join the Government Service as a clerk in the Treasury. His grasp of oral English and his lively intelligence soon marked him out for advancement. Unfortunately his zest for living the new life he had learned abroad began to outrun his means of sustaining it; and in due course this led him into error, upon which a curtain was drawn over his official career.

Some years later the Government, despairing of finding someone sufficiently competent to fill the sorely-needed post of interpreter-translator, ultimately—and only after much public debate—appointed 'Uliti to the post. He was accorded an official pardon without which he could not have been reinstated and which forgave but, as I came to know, did not quite forget his indiscretion.

'Uliti was both my mentor and right-hand man. He introduced me to some of the intricacies of Tongan language and custom. His comments on politicians, petitioners and pests, if not always objective, were pithy, enlightening and to the point. He would accept responsibility—a rare attribute at his level—and see through the administrative details of a large feast, a high school board meeting, or a complex official occasion. He also ran an admirable men's singing club, refereed football matches, and on more than one emergency occasion conveyed visiting potentates round the island with aplomb. He became the nearest thing I had to a public relations officer. He interpreted for Queens, Governor-Generals, Governors, Ambassadors, Ministers and lesser mortals. His highly developed sense of formal tact always enabled him to add in his translation any locally appropriate salutation or sentiment inadvertently omitted by a visiting speaker. He was in attendance at meetings of the Privy Council and Cabinet and thus possessed the administrative secrets of the land. His insight into the psychology of two worlds made him always an invaluable aide; and for myself I found his reliability constant and his loyalty touching. He had the ear and was the voice of all.

Among the lesser luminaries of the staff, there was a genial giant, appropriately named Taunoholo (Town Hall) who looked after the vote books impeccably and paid our monthly salaries in Tongan Treasury notes.

The correspondence clerk was a youth of faintly ingratiating enthusiasms who had also been to Australia. He tended to gaze fitfully into the blue whenever unobserved and to start guiltily when caught in the act. His less acceptable habits lay in placing an important letter in the wrong envelope (or none) and thus, at times, causing untold confusion in the further reaches of the kingdom; smoking grimy cigarettes; and contriving near-lethal combinations of whisky and gin.

The most recently appointed clerk was a convert to Mormonism and a curiously introvert youth who could take up to three days to deliver a letter fifty yards. His personality underwent a glowing metamorphosis whenever he played the trumpet in the mission band. On other occasions, he relapsed into a kind of perplexed sobriety.

For different reasons, the two most intriguing characters in the office were Vaeatangitau and Loka Mafi. The former was the filing clerk, a short, tubby little man with a Puckish sense of humour and an incongruous dago moustache. He guarded his charges with zealous care. His greatest official joy was to receive an affirmative answer to his "Shall I open a new file, Sir?" More files meant, in the long run, more spanking new steel filing cabinets. Vaeatangitau was a father of five, a Roman Catholic, and a man of substance. He possessed a wooden house and a motor-bike. Each day he rode in from the depths of Tongatapu, divesting himself on arrival of leggings, windbreaker, helmet and goggles. All that in tropical heat seemed oddly inappropriate; but they were the distinctive accoutrements portrayed in motor-cycling journals and had therefore to be worn.

Vaeatangitau was susceptible to one other eccentricity: he wrote periodic little notes to me on subjects, both personal and official, about which he was concerned. They came on scraps of used paper and were often inserted unobtrusively into some currently active file. His penchant for writing notes may have resulted from his observation of the practice of minuting: he felt that he too had better "put up his case" on paper.

I found his first missive in my inward tray on the eve of Christmas 1954:

Dear Mr. Bain,

If I hurt you, Sir, please forgive me for the sake of Xmas. Could you please buy me bottle liquor. You need not afraid of anything as I have a permit to drink only. I got the cash in hand. Thank you, Sir.

(Sgd) S. Vaeat
yr. Jr. Clk.
24.12.54

However I do not like this creating precedent to the rest.

Everyone had to possess a permit to buy or drink alcohol. This provision applied very sensibly to Tongan and European alike—sensibly, because there could then be no complaint of discrimination. The type of permit varied, however; and Vaetangitau had one which enabled him to drink beer but not to buy whisky or gin for home consumption. He had, by Christmas, already exhausted his December quota of beer and could not obtain his January allocation until the New Year. Hence the plea. Regrettably, I also did "not like this creating precedent to the rest" and, incidentally, breaking the law into the bargain. He received my comfortless "Sorry, no" with a conspiratorial grin. Our friendship remained unimpaired.

In June, His Eminence Cardinal Gilroy, Roman Catholic Archbishop of Sydney, visited Nuku'alofa for two days. The Catholic world of Tonga was agog with excited anticipation for months before. Another little note duly reached me—a more formal one this time:

S/G.

Next Monday will be the biggest feast and welcome ever extended by Catholic followers to a Visitor of my church 'Cardinal Gilroy' and am begging for leave on that day.

This day is also a big day for me in my official work but please consider Condition of Tonga and other points of views.

I am sorry that religious business has had rather a nuisance lately but I just couldn't help it, Sir.

Your filing servant,
S. Vaeatangitau
24/6/55

The Archbishop arrived on the *Tofua* from Auckland. This did mean a "big day" for the filing clerk, but I could not resist considering "Condition of Tonga and other points of views". My "filing servant" got his day off.

Then in July applications were invited to fill a vacant post of male telephone operator in the Telegraph and Telephone Department. Women were used by day but men were preferred for the solitary all-night vigil at the exchange. One applicant had been officially recommended, after interview, for the post. This informative little missive arrived as the decision was pending:

S/G.

Recommended Candidate for Male Telephone Operator

I do not wish to tell you this but I can't shut my mouth in view of the public interest, and the Government.

This person was suspended, 1946, because of such and such—
At pages 1—4—F.23/46—attached you will find the story.

S. Vaeat.

He was, of course, right. The search for a male telephone operator had to be re-opened.

At two minutes to three one afternoon, my office door opened and Loka Mafi came in. Loka was unusual insofar as he was a male stenographer; one of his principal duties was to pound out the stencilled daily news summary which we issued in English and Tongan every afternoon. He was a handsome youth, unusually slim for a Polynesian, and was an agreeable and well-spoken young man.

I had noticed that Loka frequently received visitations from sleek young maidens during office hours. Since they generally came in pairs and never seemed to be the same girls twice, it was sensible to accept Loka's story that they were bent on consultations about urgent church business, no clerical activity of any sort apparently being possible without Loka's oracular advice.

"Sir," began Loka, as I looked up, "may I have your permission to go over to the Justice Department at three o'clock for a few minutes? I have some business to do."

I reflected a moment and asked whether he had finished typing the *Daily News* which had to be distributed at four. He had finished the English version but not the Tongan.

"Why don't you finish the news and go to the Justice Department afterwards? You know the rush there always is before four o'clock."

He paused and looked mournful. The only trouble was that he had arranged to go at three.

"Well," I said testily, "I suppose neither the Justice Department nor you will be unduly inconvenienced if you go at three-thirty or whenever you have finished." And with that he retired from the scene.

Half an hour later there was a commotion in the typists' room next door. I turned a sour look on the filing clerk as he burst in, and diagnosed a request for "special-concession-just-for-me" on the grounds of his being a Hard-Working Family Man. I was wrong—Vaeatangitau was also the office intelligence agent.

"Do you know something, Sir?" he asked.

"No," I answered wearily, "all I know is that there is a confounded noise next door. What is it?"

"It's Loka Mafi," he said, beaming from ear to ear. "He's just got married!"

"Got married!" I echoed, unbelievingly. "Bring him in."

We were joined a minute later by Loka, sheepish but otherwise unchanged. "What's this I hear about your having been married?"

"That's right," said Loka, and giggled. "Ten minutes ago," he added, a little defiantly I thought.

"You mean to tell me that that is why you wanted to go to the Justice Department at three o'clock?"

"Yes, Sir," said Loka, reproachfully.

"Then why in heaven's name didn't you say so?"

Loka's head drooped and in the emotional state arising from recent events in his life, could find no answer.

A further thought struck me. "Loka, I thought you were a good Catholic. What's the idea of getting married in a registry office? Is your wife a Catholic?"

"No," he replied "She's a Wesleyan and the Bishop is marrying us again after I finish work today . . ."

"Go home now." My voice seemed unusually loud. "Go home and somebody else can finish the news today."

Next morning he was seated as usual behind his typewriter. I called him into my office. He looked even more sheepish.

"Loka," I began apologetically, "I am afraid that in the excitement of yesterday afternoon I forgot to tell you to take a few days off. It's the normal thing when you get married."

He smiled. "Thank you very much, but I'd just as soon carry on working. There's a lot to be done here today."

"So there is, so there is," I beamed indulgently. "But what about your wife? Where is she? Doesn't she want a honeymoon?"

"She's at home. She understands. I told her I would be busy today. She's a typist too, you know," he added with a touch of professional pride.

"Oh, well," I reflected, rebuffed, "you ought to know best I suppose."

And as Loka went out, I crashed my pencil point on the desk pad.

6 Perspective

I NEVER counted them, but the statisticians state categorically that the Kingdom of Tonga comprises some 150 islands lying within the great Polynesian belt of the Pacific Ocean which also includes Hawaii, Samoa, the Cooks, Tahiti, Niue and the Ellice Islands. The three main groups—Tongatapu in the south, Ha'apai in the centre, and Vava'u in the north—cover an area of 270 square miles between eighteen and twenty degrees south of the equator. The islands fall into two distinct types: the western line is volcanic and hilly, while the eastern strip is coralline and flat.

To the latter category belongs Falcon Island, which has also been called "Jack-in-the-Box-Island" because of its propensity for doing the disappearing trick. Some time ago, the sight of clouds of smoke and steam rising from the ocean's surface in the direction of Falcon Island gave rise to the report that it was about to emerge again. But in fact Falcon still rests discreetly beneath the Pacific. An over-imaginative tourist company listed the possibility of seeing Falcon appear and disappear as one of the attractions of a visit to Tonga: they did not add that the island was last visible in 1942.

Tongan history can be traced back through the royal lineage to the tenth century; and there were until the nineteenth century separate lines of spiritual kings, the Tu'i Tonga, and temporal kings, the Tu'i Kanokupolu and Tu'i Ha'atakalaua. The first of the spiritual kings, 'Ahoeitu, lived about the time of Alfred the Great; and today his name and those of his descendants are taught in Tongan schools as the names of the kings of England are taught to students of English history.

The Tu'i Tonga were lords of the soil and enjoyed divine honours by virtue of their supposedly immortal origin. Later, the temporal line of kings emerged and it is from these that the present royal dynasty descends. By the middle of the nineteenth century, the kingdom had been united under George Tupou I, the first Christian king and the father of modern Tonga. And so were swept aside the old beliefs and the customary institutions that depended on them. Today, every Tongan is both Christian and literate, and Tonga is the only land where the Methodist Church is the State church.

The 76,000 subjects of the King of Tonga live within the framework of a written constitution which has remained essentially unchanged since its inception in 1875. With its forthright pronouncements and what might be regarded elsewhere as quaint anachronisms, the constitution bestows upon the lords, squires and commoners freedom from slavery and religious duress, freedom of speech, and assurance of the equitable administration of the law for all. The person of the monarch it declares to be sacred.

The capital, Nuku'alofa, is not a metropolis, but it has a distinctive character of its own: and, like the kingdom as a whole, everything is in miniature. It is only a few steps from the wharf to the Post Office and Treasury, the Premier's Office and Police Station, the Magistrates' Court and the Lands Department. Over the road and beyond the public green along the foreshore are the Palace grounds. In five minutes you can reach the mal'e which encircles the royal burial ground and tombs. In doing so, you will have entered and left the business centre of the town where Manchester and Hong Kong cottons hang from little windows and coconut-leaf baskets of pineapples, taro and tapioca patiently await a buyer. The streets have no gutters for the town is completely flat. Instead, the centre of the road is raised like a hump bridge and the tropical rain slides away past the low props of the wooden buildings which for two hundred yards constitute the centre of the capital. But though it is all on a small scale, the same elements of living—of love and hate, of sickness and health, of friendship and jealousy, of sadness and joy—all make up a pattern of life which in these essentials is not very different from that elsewhere. Where difference does lie is in emphasis. A chiefly birth may involve customary tributes from hundreds, while the death of a high chief will have its effect on the daily lives of vast numbers of people. The higher the rank of the person who is born, marries or dies, the wider the scope of personal and customary involvement. Then there is the abundance of hospitality, the dancing and singing, the feasts and the generosity which never fail to impress the visitor and to warm the heart of the pseudo-cynical old hand.

The seventy-odd miles of road through the coconut and banana plantations of the island are good, but there are uncatalogued driving hazards. A people accustomed to the free movement of village life regard traffic control as largely irrelevant to road conditions. There is a yellow line painted down the centre of the pathless main street. It is used sometimes by cyclists to see whether they can ride straight along it without falling off. This works so long as there is no one coming the other way. If there is, chaos can result, for there are Tongans who seem to ride a bicycle or drive a car with ears and eyes closed to the surrounding world while doing so.

The town has frequent stop signs, but it has been said that they are all in the main streets and not on the side ones. This has the unusual but perhaps the desired effect of translating the by-ways into highways and vice versa. At two intersections in the town, traffic policemen are stationed from eight in the morning until five in the afternoon. Normally, they are dressed in khaki uniforms and ten-gallon hats; but on important occasions such as the arrival of the monthly steamer from New Zealand, they are resplendent in white tunics and *valas*, blue hats and brown sandals. They work under miniature band rotundas painted in the Tongan colours of red and white. And when a car appears, their arms switch sharply right or left with frantic precision.

In the country there is no official speed limit, but there are natural hazards. Tonga, as the world knows, has an abundance of pigs, none of which is amenable to captivity; and you cannot drive for more than a mile or two into the outlying villages without an old sow and some of her offspring dashing from out of the coconuts into the centre of the road just when you've put your foot down and are off at the gay old speed of thirty miles an hour. Adequate speed control is thus ensured at no expense or apparent effort on the part of authority.

There were few stores of consequence in Nuku'alofa, other

than those owned by the European commercial firms and traders. An exception was that created by Holika Naufahu, a young man of enterprise and ideas rather more advanced than those of many of his contemporaries. Holika had acquired a piece of land in the middle of town, collected some timber, paint and glass and begun lively correspondence with exporters of textiles and piece-goods in Japan, Hong Kong and Lancashire. He sold his imported corned beef a few pence cheaper than his next-door neighbour and filled his windows with unusual goods. Soon the prosperous little trading post he called "The People's Store" began to cause come concern to established business; and Holika thrived on the unrest of former monopoly.

Astute though he was, Holika had overlooked one important point. The land on which he had his store was leased to him; and, unfortunately, the lease soon ran out. Protests against throttling the emergence of a potentially great emporium proved of no avail to an adamant landlord, whom Holika darkly hinted was in the camp of his rivals. So he was faced with removal or closure; and he began to look round for somewhere to go.

Then he had a piece of luck. Almost directly across the main road was a small vacant plot, the backyard, in fact, of a local commercial magnate—ice-cream manufacturer, billiard saloon proprietor, garage owner and Representative of the People in the Legislative Assembly. Not without good business instinct, this realist saw in Holika a better partner than rival and offered his vacant plot. Holika signed up and began to examine the physical problem of transferring his stock and premises.

Elsewhere a gang of carpenters would have demolished and re-erected the building over the way. Not so in Tonga where the populace is not unaccustomed to finding whole wooden houses disappear overnight and materialise intact next morning, a mile or two down the road. So, at five o'clock one afternoon, Holika collected all his friends, about twenty coconut logs, a truck and some rope and began to shift his shop. He placed the logs under the store and whacked away the concrete foundations. With much sweat and conflicting instructions from elder statesmen, the building more-or-less gently dropped on to the logs. Holika laced up the truck, started the engine and set off, shop and all, into the main street. After every foot or so of forward movement, the logs at the back were rushed around to the front in a continuous belt-like relay. Passers-by were conscripted into the gang and soon the house was astride and blocking the whole street. Traffic went another way and the policeman on point duty twenty yards off cheerfully abandoned his post to offer official advice. The trickiest bit was the 180-degree angle turn when the job was half-way through. Even this did not cause Holika undue worry as his store strained and groaned its way across the sealed roadway.

Next morning "The People's Store" was open again for business on the other side of the street. Two days later it might never have been anywhere else. But I shall not forget one thing: I have seen officers of the law controlling strange contraptions and beasts in a number of thoroughfares of the world, but not before or since have I witnessed a policeman solemnly waving on a shop.

Nuku'alofa is also the seat of Government. Every Friday morning at ten o'clock the Privy Council met at the Palace, presided over by Her Majesty the Queen. Despatch boxes and policy papers did the rounds—even in the escapist atmosphere of the Friendly Islands. When the Queen was away, her elder son, Prince Tungi, was Prince Regent. He was also the Premier and three mornings a week he met with the Cabinet which, with one exception, consisted of Tongan Ministers. Both the Privy Council and Cabinet now have an all-Tongan membership. The Ministers of the Crown, including the Governors of Ha'apai and Vava'u when they are in Nuku'alofa, also sit as Privy Councillors and Cabinet Ministers.

The Legislative Assembly is the law-making body, although Privy Council has limited powers to pass ordinances between sessions of the Assembly. The five Ministers and two Governors are official members, the others being seven Representatives of the Nobles and a similar number of Representatives of the People. There are thirty-three landed estates of the nobility in Tonga, and the incumbents of these, which include most of the Ministers, elect their representatives every three years. At the same time the "people" do likewise, all literate Tongans, other than nobles, who pay taxes and are over the age of twenty-one being eligible to vote. The Assembly thus virtually consists of a joint Upper and Lower House.

Since the Representatives of the People have been known to vote *en bloc* against the Government bench, the nobles hold the balance of power; normally they vote with the Government, but sometimes they do not. A Government defeat then follows.

"Apart from the possible exception of Switzerland," Prince Tungi once remarked, "Tonga is, I believe, the only country in the world where a responsible Government is in a perpetual minority in the Legislature; but it has comfort in the knowledge that even if it is outvoted on a material point it does not go out of office!"

The reason is that the Ministers, although constitutionally responsible, are appointed during the pleasure of the Sovereign. They are not politicians in the sense understood elsewhere. Since they are often chiefs in their own right, the authority of a written constitution is reinforced by the traditions of a thousand years of Tongan life where rank is authority and authority has customary rank.

The Tongan sees chiefly exercise of authority within the machinery of present-day government as both logical and fitting. An important element in his character is respect for the chiefs, and this influences his life profoundly; it dictates his manner of living and makes social demands on his everyday intercourse. To merit this respect, the chiefs must observe a standard of propriety and conduct befitting their chiefly position; and it is probably respect which is the ultimate foundation of the love each Tongan bears for his sovereign and the Royal Family.

The continuity of his spiritual and temporal history gives the Tongan an unquestioning belief in the security of his country. Nationalism is a factor of public life only insofar as it is to be maintained with dignity and pride—the understandable pride of the people of the only remaining independent Polynesian kingdom.

Except for external affairs and defence, the country is autonomous; it has its own paper money and postage stamps and when a Tongan goes overseas he carries with him a Tongan and not a British passport. The Kingdom has thus gained something of the best of two worlds—on the one hand, self-government and virtual independence; and on the other, the friendly protection of Great Britain within the orbit of the Commonwealth. Since the Constitution also forbids the alienation of land to non-Tongans, there has been an absence of land-ownership and racial problems. Overall, the national unity and confidence which has been fostered may well be the envy of less favoured lands. It is certainly a lasting tribute to the foresight of the Tongan leaders of the past.

7 The Government of Tonga v. *Vogue* Magazine

THE Tongan is indulgent of European ignorance of his customs, but he is sensitive to public misrepresentation of his way of life. When this affects the Royal Family or the nobles, Tongan determination to put right the wrong can become rigid to the point of obstinacy. There was a case in point shortly after the coronation of Queen Elizabeth in June, 1953.

Tungi had been sent a cutting from the American *Vogue* magazine. This purported to report the goings-on at a coronation garden party given by the Duke and Duchess of Marlborough in Blenheim Palace at which Queen Salote was present. During the course of the article, this statement appeared:

> At this summer's garden party, among the famous and witty, the admirable and startling Queen Salote of Tonga is said to have said on recognising British regiments represented among the guests: "Some of their forebears had the honour of being the main dish for some of my ancestors".

Tungi, who was Prince Regent at the time, was incensed to find his mother so reported and shortly afterwards raised the matter at a meeting of the Privy Council. As a result, Deputy Premier Havea Tu'iha'ateiho was charged with writing to Queen Salote to ascertain the accuracy or otherwise of her reported statement.

Havea did so, the Queen having by this time reached Auckland in the course of her journey back to Tonga from Europe. There was, he said, amidst the great and joyous tales of Her Majesty's welcome in England but one disturbing report which had caused the chiefs and loyal subjects of Her Majesty pained concern.

Havea then quoted the report and finished up by saying that while Privy Council was positive that no such words had been uttered by their Queen, it would nonetheless be gratified to be reassured that this was so.

Queen Salote was upset; and indeed anyone having the remotest knowledge of her deep sense of propriety and the fitness of things would have known that she could never have made the statement attributed to her. And that, of course, was why she was upset. In Tonga a whole world of Polynesian pride, sovereignty and past rivalry with their predominantly Melanesian Fijian neighbours was offended at such misrepresentation of historical fact. For all the centuries of rivalry, wars and dynastic struggles for power both within and outside his country, the Tongan had never become a compulsive eater of human flesh and always decried the practice.

I had been in Tonga only eight weeks. It was insufficient for a sensitive understanding of these issues.

As her Ministers fully expected, the Queen repudiated the statement. She had seen no newspaper men, all of whom had been received by her staff. In any event, she concluded, "Polynesians were not cannibals; but even if they had been, it would hardly have been the appropriate time to remind my hosts of such a thing after the magnificent welcome they extended to me."

The Queen's letter was placed before the Privy Council which asked the Deputy Premier to consult the Government legal adviser about what action should be taken. The latter, a hard-bitten New Zealand second world war veteran, took a terse view of ministerial concern. After a lengthy outline of the legal position as he saw it, he advocated forgive and forget; and I expressed myself as being in agreement with his view.

The Privy Council, however, was not. Had I understood more at the time, I would have known why. When the honourable gentlemen again found the matter on their agenda, they decided that the Deputy Premier should write to the Secretary of State for the Colonies in London for further advice as to what action they could take. This was duly done through the British Agent and Consul. He in turn referred the letter to the Governor of Fiji to whom, as Consul-General for the Western Pacific at that time, he was responsible. At the end of October, the Tonga Government was informed that the Governor had discussed the matter with Queen Salote on her way through Fiji on her return to Tonga. He understood that the issue would be further considered in Tonga before the Secretary of State was brought into the picture.

In the meantime, Tungi had gone to New Zealand; and it was not until the middle of December that Privy Council decided that a letter should be sent to *Vogue* saying that the statement was incorrect and untrue and might a correction please be published. I pondered on this for a while and finally decided to return the papers yet again to Privy Council. The legal adviser had reiterated his previous advice that if *Vogue* declined to publish an apology there would be an obligation on the Government to take action against the magazine the only results of which would be unwanted publicity and considerable expense. In any event, the remark was probably published as a joke and had long since been forgotten by the publishers and readers of *Vogue*.

It had *not* long since been forgotten by the Ministers of the Tongan Crown whose instructions six weeks later at the end of January amounted to get on with it and stop procrastinating. So, on the 9th February, we did, pointing out to *Vogue* that the statement was historically untrue since no members of any British Regiment were known to have been victims of cannibalism in Tonga.

The result was as handsome an apology as anyone could expect to receive, although *Vogue* did remind the Premier that their story had made it clear that the Queen was "*said* to have said . . ." In the April 1954 issue of *Vogue* appeared a caption "Correction—and Apologies to a Queen". The alleged remark was reproduced below with the gist of the Government letter; then a regret for the misquotation, and apologies to Her Majesty the Queen of Tonga for the error.

I presented the tearsheet of the correction to Privy Council on the 12th April and hoped for their recognition of a tactical victory. And so there was, the Ministers accepting the apology and going so far as to ask that a letter of thanks be sent to *Vogue*. This was duly done at the end of April and after the British Consul had been advised that no further action was contemplated by the Government of Tonga, the file was at last put away after a life of over eight months. It was my first real insight into the Tongan mind.

8 Whale of a Time

THE envelope was lying on my desk pad when I arrived at the office. The pencilled writing was unfamiliar, but there was nothing remarkable in that since I had been in Tonga only a few weeks. I hadn't yet had time to be able to distinguish the calligraphy of all my local correspondents. Inside the envelope was a brief note written on a sheet of paper torn out of a school exercise book.

Dear Sir,

Will you be good enough to lend me £1 to buy whale.

Very sorry to worry you and I trust you will not regard me nuisance.

Thanking you for your kindness,

Yours respectfully,
Moses Havili

P.S. Please charge for milk.

The signatory was my milkman, a genial rogue who had supplied milk to a number of my predecessors. Every six months or so over the years he had been threatened with withdrawal of patronage whenever the proportion of water to milk exceeded reasonable limits. Voluble written explanations always followed these tiresome complaints from his clients. Appropriately, his second name meant "wind".

The possibility of my milkman being indebted to me instead of the other way intrigued me only because I was new to Tonga. I had already begun to discover that many of the conventions of other lands had a slight Alice-in-Wonderland flavour in the Friendly Islands. In this case my hesitation came from experience in Fiji of the predilection for credit and for storing up monthly debts far in excess of what was likely to come in at the end of the month. I didn't particularly want to start a chain reaction, but milk was scarce—even with water in it—and I was curious to find out what was meant by "£1 to buy whale". So Havili got his pound.

Where the milkman was proposing to acquire a whale—and how much one cost in Tonga—I hadn't a notion. Unless he had some singularly gullible customers to whom he had addressed pleas for greater financial aid than mine, I couldn't see his coming closer to a whale than a chunk off the rump.

And that, I learned, was precisely what he was after. A whale had been caught the night before and brought into the harbour of Nuku'alofa. Out on the reef, it was being slowly dismembered and cut up for sale to the local populace for whom whale meat is as delectable a delicacy as Christmas turkey in Britain. I am ever indebted to Havili for his irresistible *cri de coeur* because it was responsible for setting me off in search of this tale of whaling as it is carried out by the Friendly Islanders.

Walk along the palm-studded fringe of the harbour at Nuku'alofa on any day between the months of July and October, and you may well come across a gathering of colourful, excited people watching the arrival of a small launch displaying an outsize black and white flag. An hour or two later, the roads into the country will be thronged with men, women and children clutching iron hooks on which thick hunks of rich raw meat are strung. In many homes that night a hilarious family feast will be held; while by the seashore a rancid smell lingers inescapably in the salt air—the smell of a dead and gutted whale whose great bones lie bare on the reef in the moonlight.

Fifty yards away from our house in Nuku'alofa lived the remarkable Walter Cook whose family history embraces whaling in Tonga as the thrilling, hazardous operation it was everywhere 200 years ago. It all had a simple, fortuitous beginning.

In the latter part of the nineteenth century, a flourishing and profitable whaling industry developed along the coasts of New Zealand. If the methods then were primitive, the rewards were lucrative. They needed to be, for chasing a thumping great whale with a hand harpoon in an open rowing boat was no task for the timorous. Engaged in this business was Walter Cook's father who, as an adventurous young man of twenty-five decided to try his luck in the warmer waters of the islands north of his own country.

In July 1885, he signed on a three-master schooner bound north-east for Tonga. On the deck were ranged the iron whale pots which were gradually filled with oil as the voyage progressed. Lashed to the sides of the schooner were the whale boats which went out in search each day from the mother ship. In the first week of August, the schooner sailed past Nukuʻalofa and headed north through the reef passages to the sheltered water between Foa and Lifuka in Haʻapai where another more famous Cook had landed just over a hundred years before. When the ship was safely achored, the crew got down to the main purpose of the expedition and at dawn each day the whale boats set off by sail and oar.

The catch that year was good. The pots were filled more quickly than had been expected and the crew made ready to sail again to the south before the hurricane season began in November. Two days before they were due to weigh anchor, an unseasonable gale sprang up from the south-east, scudded across the open seaway and smashed into the unprepared ship. It was Sunday and most of the crew were on shore. By the time they had assembled at the beach, the schooner was already fast on the reef. Only one of the whale boats had escaped damage, while the schooner itself was beyond local repair. She was sold by auction—a whimsical method of disposing of a ship—a few weeks later. Arrangements were made for the repatriation of the captain and his crew by the monthly passenger steamer from New Zealand. They sailed back home in melancholy mood and out of the story of whaling in Tonga. Behind them they left a scuppered ship, a shattered business and one member of the crew. Seduced perhaps by the luxuriant charm of Haʻapai, Cook had decided not to return to his homeland.

For a time he worked for the new owner of the whale boat which began to carry copra between the islands of Haʻapai. Then, when he had accumulated sufficient money, he bought the boat and the whaling gear. The business consisted at first of the extraction of oil and small shipments of it to New Zealand in the old metal pots. Cook stayed on in Tonga, devoted to whaling and to the people of his adoption; and it was not long before he married a young girl of Ha'apai.

Walter Cook was the sixth son of that marriage, and when I first met him in 1954 he was in his early fifties. He in turn, although retaining his New Zealand citizenship, had married a Tongan and produced an impressively handsome family of six boys and two girls. He was a gentle, modest man, meticulously rearing his family within the framework of the church, and the customs and language of the land of his birth. His unexpectedly blue eyes reflected the sea and the edges were crinkled with the sun and the wind. The skill, resourcefulness and enterprise of the father had remained alive in the son.

Before he married, Walter Cook's crew consisted of anyone he could persuade to go out with him in his power-less whale boat. When I met him, it consisted of five of his sons, the youngest of whom was fifteen. The precise nature of their methods was a jealously guarded family secret and it took some time before Cook would tell me about them. Each member of the crew is assigned to and specially trained for his own part in the chase, the kill and the capture. Courage, reliability, timing and initiative in emergency are essential in each member. During the season, Cook normally sets out from Nuku'alofa in early morning. His equipment is the essence of primitive simplicity—harpoon, rope, long spears, whale spades and knives. The harpoon is a three-foot length of iron, steel being useless, Cook maintains, because of a tendency to snap under strain. It has a single razor-sharp barbed point. Attached to it is a piece of iron piping to which in turn a wooden handle is fixed. With a special unbreakable knot which he claims to have evolved for the purpose, Cook ties a 200-fathom length of rope on the handle. There is no ring at the end of the handle, so that an ordinary bowline, for example, is impracticable. The breaking point of the rope is a weight of about three tons. Since Cook estimates that his whales average between forty and sixty tons, I began to wonder how he ever got one home and at the same time kept crew and boat intact.

"The first essential when a whale is sighted," he told me, "is to ensure that he does not in turn see us. If he does, we lose him because he immediately dives and runs away. Now the whales we catch in these waters are all of the hump-back variety and from long experience I can tell from the position of the hump on the back of the whale whether we have been sighted or not. If the whale turns slightly to look back, the hump shifts position. When that happens, we stop and consider what we did wrong. You see, we have to sail up from behind as closely as possible without being seen by the whale. When we are about thirty yards away I hand over the tiller to my eldest son, go to the front of the boat and stand ready with the harpoon. As soon as we are eighteen or twenty feet off, away goes the harpoon. It weighs about ten pounds and that's about as far as I can manage with the rope as well. I try to get the harpoon as near to the head of the hump as possible and if I am lucky, in it goes up to the full three feet of the piping. Then the fun really begins."

I remarked, in awe at anyone who could approach a fifty-ton whale so close and stick a piece of iron into it, that I supposed the fun did.

"At exactly the same moment as the harpoon strikes," Cook continued in as matter-of-fact a voice as you would find in an Oxford Junior Common Room, "the sail comes down and the oars go out. As you can imagine, the whale goes berserk as soon as he is struck and we need all our wits. Out he thrashes with his tail like a bucking stallion. One strike with fifty tons of maddened whale behind it and that's the end of our boat. I've had to swim for my life twice from the outside of Malinoa to 'Atata."

I closed my eyes and visualised the truly "shark-infested waters" through which Cook swam five miles to safety.

"Now the purpose of the harpoon is not to kill but to hold the whale. When the harpoon strikes, down he goes to about twenty fathoms, threshing the surface of the sea in a frenzy as he dives and pulling the boat along behind him like an aquaplane. The nose of the boat goes up and the spray blinds the helmsman who cannot see the bow. Off goes the rope in a wild flurry and we hope we've brought enough.

"The whale's first rush generally lasts about three minutes; then the speed slackens and we get in a little rope as the whale comes up to ten or fifteen feet and perhaps to the surface for air. If all has gone according to plan, the tough, weary business of playing the whale begins—tough, because it's hard work and we never know when a rush will occur; weary, because it may take anything from twenty minutes to eight hours. I once harpooned a whale at nine in the morning. We still hadn't got him to the surface by nightfall, so I had to cut the rope and let him go. I couldn't take the risk after dark."

It was a comforting reflection that Cook thought something too hazardous to attempt. He was at least human.

So over a period of many hours in most cases, the struggle continues. Rush, slacken; rest, row and tighten. At length, when the whale comes up for air about fifteen feet from the boat and its half-exhausted crew, the first spear is flung to the heart. A second spear, attached to a light rope is thrown, retrieved and thrown again perhaps twenty times. Each time it flies to the whale, the harpoon rope is slackened in case a last desperate rush is made which would sink the boat. Then comes the blood spouting into the waves; and with the blood, the sharks, the vultures of death at sea. The climax is at hand and the whale, fighting madly in the throes of expiry, may achieve one last half-crazed thresh in the few remaining minutes of its life which might smash the boat to pulp. That is the most dangerous moment of all.

"When the whale is dead," Cook went on, "we must be quick to pull the rope right in so that he is tied firmly to the side of the boat. If we are too slow, the whale sinks and all our effort goes for nothing. We can never get him up again. Sometimes the whale begins to sink before we have quite brought him alongside. When this happens, the boat, of course, sinks too, but we don't slacken the rope until the water starts to come in over the sides. We heave with a rising wave until we've finally got him beside the boat.

"The next job is to stitch up the gaping mouth to prevent the water getting in and causing the whale to sink. One of my boys goes over the side with a short sharp spade to make a hole in the jaw about three or four feet from the mouth. A rope is pressed through the hole, across the inside of the mouth, down round the bottom of the jaw and up over the head where it is tied. While this is going on

—and it takes some minutes—the rest of my family keep off the sharks! When a whale dies, it sometimes turns over on its back and then someone has to dive overboard and turn him over before the mouth can be sewn up. Finally, the whale is lashed securely to the boat, its head always at the bow.

"All that remains is for the big square black and white flag to be hoisted. As soon as the flag is sighted from the shore or by a passing vessel, a launch comes from Nuku'alofa and tows us, whale and all, back to the harbour."

"Was there a reason why you chose a black and white flag as your signal of victory?" I asked.

"Yes," he said, and his eyes twinkled, "there was. You will have noticed that the top of the flag is black and the bottom is white. That's the same as the whale—black back and white belly. I'm rather proud of that idea."

A nice thought indeed, with a good deal more than that to be proud of. Twelve to fifteen whales a season in that way isn't bad going, even if since 1952 Cook has used dynamite to kill the whale when it is being played. The charge is placed in a pipe, the fuse is lit and timed accurately with a throw at the whale's head. The pipe explodes under the water. Sometimes one shot is enough and the whale is killed instantly. For each whale, Cook is allowed ten pounds weight of dynamite. He will probably use five pounds and keep five pounds in reserve. If the whale sinks to the bottom, he puts the reserve charge in a container, then lowers and explodes it under the whale. This is normally sufficient to shift the whale from the bed of the ocean so that it can be pulled up.

My "£1 to buy whale" had been money well spent. And if it hadn't been for the strange chance of a freak gale over seventy years ago and the resulting wreck of a New Zealand three-master, the Friendly Islands would have lacked of one of their most unusual and courageous families.

9 Wine, Women and Song

THE Tongan is an inveterate conversationalist, a natural orator and a critical judge of public speaking. The preamble to formal oratory follows a set pattern with salutations to an array of chiefly personages before the speech itself begins. The rolling cadences which follow may go on interminably without the speaker seeming to be aware or to care whether his audience is listening or not. No one bothers to stop eating at a feast to listen to the speeches.

In informal discussion, the Tongan is humorous, perceptive and earthy. A joke is rewarded with rich peals of laughter; and satirical comment is relished. The evening social life of the village centres round the bowl of *kava*, the thirst-relieving brown liquid which refreshes the palate and loosens the tongue.

There are various methods of preparing it in the South Pacific. In Tonga, pieces of the root are pounded on a smooth flat stone (*makatokalalo*) with a smaller stone (*makatoka'olunga*); the pulp is then placed in a circular wooden bowl (*kumete* or *tanoa*), water added, and the mixture strained with strands of fibre from the *fau* (hibiscus) tree until the desired solution is obtained. *Kava* is served ceremonially or informally according to the occasion and drunk from polished half-coconut shells. It has a cleansing after-effect on the palate and is pleasantly thirst-quenching on a hot day. It is at once the champagne and *vin ordinaire* of the South Pacific. No formal occasion can begin before the ceremonial libation has been dispensed; and in the evening the lure of the *kava* bowl is the Polynesian equivalent of the village pub in Britain. Around it gossip is exchanged and the fabric of domestic life dissected. Wit and song intermingle with wisdom and banter.

Ceremonials are the framework of Tongan society. The protocol for each is laid down in strict accord with ancient custom and tradition; and they have lasting significance for a people who trace back their history for a thousand years. The most solemn gathering is the Royal *Kava* Ring. Here the Sovereign is always present. The traditional order of sitting in a great outdoor egg-shaped circle is as rigid and inviolable as any at other ancient courts. *Kava* ceremonies may be held to mark the bestowal of the seasonal first-fruits to a chief; the opening of a school; or birth, marriage and death. On all these occasions every Tongan present wears a *ta'ovala* the plaited grass mat worn round the waist to express humility in the presence of persons of higher rank. No Tongan is properly dressed without a mat over his clothes; and it does the same for him as a jacket and tie for a man, or a hat and gloves for a woman, in European society. But there is a great deal more to it than this and it was Queen Salote who first explained it to me.

"There are *ta'ovala* of varying degree of customary significance," she said. "For instance, the *ta'ovala* worn at the dedication of a new boat is made of the bark of the *fau* tree; that worn at funerals covers the body from the chest to the ankles and is of coarse texture; the wedding *ta'ovala* is a fine cream-coloured mat of silky smoothness wrapped round and round the bride. The *ta'ovala* I wore when I met Queen Elizabeth on Her Majesty's arrival in Tonga was six hundred years old. Worshipped in the thirteenth century as a symbol of the ancient gods, the mat belonged to the chiefly family of Malupo on the island of 'Uiha. The head of this family was descended from a brother of the twentieth Tu'i Tonga. When King Tupouto'a (my great-great-great-grandfather) came to the throne in 1802, the title of *Lalanga'a 'Ulukilupetea* meaning 'the weaving of 'Ulukilupetea' (Tupouto'a's mother) was bestowed on it. It was worn only on great ceremonial occasions by Tupouto'a himself, his son George Tupou I, and my father George Tupou II. I wore the *Lalanga'a 'Ulukilupetea* for the first time when I was installed as sovereign at my *kava* ring in 1918.

"Each line of kings had its own ceremonial mats which were carefully preserved from generation to generation. In fact, our history is written, not in books, but in our mats. I have in my possession a number of historic *ta'ovala* including those from the sacred Tu'i Tonga line. It was fitting therefore that the Royal Visit to Tonga of the Queen of Great Britain and Head of the

Commonwealth should be recorded in our history in this mat which I regard as the Tongan counterpart of the Coronation Chair of King Edward I."

Part of the family tree of the possessors of this unique Polynesian heirloom is reproduced below.

MALUPO
(descendant of a brother of the 20th Tu'i Tonga)
(about 1400)

SIU'ULUA
(daughter)
|
'ULUKILUPETEA
(daughter)
|
TUPOUTO'A
(17th Tu'i Kanokupolu)
(1812–1820)

PRINCESS HALAEVALU MATA'AHO	KING GEORGE TUPOU I* (19th Tu'i Kanokupolu) (1845–1893)

PRINCESS SALOTE PILOLEVU	PRINCE DAVID 'UNGA
FATAFEHI-TOUTAI TU'IPELEHAKE married	PRINCESS FUSIPALA

KING GEORGE TUPOU II
(1893–1918)
(20th Tu'i Kanokupolu)
|
QUEEN SALOTE TUPOU III
(1918–1965)
|
KING TAUFA'AHAU TUPOU IV
(1965–)

* The 18th Tu'i Kanokupolu was Tupouto'a's uncle, succession in the Kanokupolu line of kings until George Tupou I's constitution being by appointment immediately before the death of the reigning Tu'i Kanokupolu.

"The *kafa* or sinnet cord I wore round the *ta'ovala*," continued Queen Salote, "was given to my son Tungi before the death of Alipate 'Uluafioetau, who was my husband's uncle; it belonged to one of the old kings, Tupoulahisi'i, the tenth Tu'i Kanokupolu; I am the twenty-first of that line of our dynasty.

"When I returned to the Palace the day after the Royal Visit, I noticed that one ashtray had not been emptied. I called one of the staff and asked why it had not been taken away. He replied that he had not wished to do that because it had been used by the Duke of Edinburgh. In Tongan custom anything personally used by Royalty cannot be used by anybody else. I said 'Well, you had better wrap it up before someone takes it away and washes it.' So the ashtray was wrapped up—with the ash of the Duke's cigarette —and put away. And so, too, have the mats which will hold the story of the two days the Royal couple spent within the Palace."

The human race is fortunate in that we are not all equally attracted by the same man or woman. While there is a certain amount of overlapping—sufficient to keep the marriage counsellors in business—some are conservative in appreciation of beauty in other races. Beauty certainly lies in the eye of the Tongan beholder, for his concept of feminine elegance is unlikely to gain acceptance on Miami Beach. Basil Thomson described it like this in 1902:

> The perfect woman must be fat—that is most imperative—and her neck must be short; she must have no waist, and if nature has cursed her with that defect she must disguise it with draperies, or submit to be 'miscalled' in the streets of Nuku-'alofa; her bust, hips and thighs must be colossal. The woman who possesses all these perfections will be esteemed chieflike and elegant, and her nose will not matter, though, if she have that organ flat to the face, she will be painting the lily . . .
>
> . . . There chanced to be an illustrated paper on the table, and when I showed the women the wasp-waisted ladies in the fashion plates, they chuckled with amusement and derision. The King, whom I afterwards asked for a definition of female beauty, confirmed all they said, and added a philosophical explanation

of his own. He said that the human eye demanded a sufficiency in the things presented to it; if they were insufficient, it found them ugly. The Tongan dress did not conceal the form as does [*sic*] the European; consequently Tongan ladies were expected to be satisfying in respect of the portions of their anatomy which are exposed to view.

We may be content with a simpler explanation. In days gone by the chiefly women got more to eat than their inferiors, and *enbonpoint* became a chiefly attribute. This mark of high birth being once stereotyped, men chose their wives accordingly, and the Tongan dames will grow stouter with every generation. It is not a pleasing prospect . . .

Thomson may not have been entirely right, but it is true that chiefly Tongan men and women are taller and more generously built than their more humble compatriots. A Tongan friend once described for me the cycle of feminine family life. This is what he wrote:

Our estimation of beauty is different from the European's points of view. To choose a wife one may look upon each of the following—a chiefly family, or a prosperous good family, which is the average point of view of wise men. But concerning the Tongan youth, no, he is after the beauty of the lady concerned. The Tongans consider a girl beautiful if she is not thin and feeble. They rather see a girl with graceful big whitish legs and arms than to see a beautiful face with very thin, black limbs.

When a baby is born, the first question asked by the mother is this: "Is it a baby girl?" If it happens to be a baby girl, the mother is said to be lucky, not only because of the help that she expects to receive from her little baby girl when she grows up, but because the mother herself is looking forward to the far future, when her little girl will marry a fine gentleman.

The little girl is told not to run about with naked skin; her hair will be attended regularly; every piece of *tapa* or material will be put aside for her dress for Sunday services. As a matter

Preparations for a feast

A male dancer

A sitting dance for women

Dancing girls of Ha'apai

of fact, wearing of new dress to Church on Sunday was a custom handling over from the past since contact with the Europeans. This is true in modern time. A girl would rather stay at home on Sunday than to visit the church with an old but clean dress.

Now the little girl is grown into girlhood and as she grows she is instructed in certain actions, she is told not to do this or that. All this is taken in case her beauty is spoilt. The girl must wear long *vala* (underskirt) to cover her legs almost to the ground. She will not be allowed to sit cross-legged as the boys do. She is told not to place her elbows or knuckles on any hard solid objects. The mother is taking all these cares to keep her little girl's skin smooth. To stop having rough spots on the little girl's skin, the usual practice is to rub the skin with a mixture of candlenut oil, nut grass oil and three or four leaves or flowers of the most scented plants chewed by the mother or the girl herself.

When once a girl is beginning to do this type of thing, she is then in the courtship stage no matter how old she is. Gentlemen will be seen hanging round her house at night wishing to court her. At night when gentlemen come to entertain the girl, the mother will not go to bed, but she will go and peep from some hidden corner. Now begins the hard life of the mother. She will keep watch every now and then. She will not allow her daughter to walk with a friend even in the day time. If the girl wishes to go to a dance, the mother will let her go, but she (mother) will do the escorting. She will not be allowed to do any work that may strain her muscles. Her manner of receiving visitors is also taught by the mother. All these precautions are taken because of the final day, which is the Wedding Day. The final decision comes on the wedding day when all the secrets of her beauty are revealed.

On the day of the presentation of the Tongan wealths, the girl, for the first time, will wear all the necessary finely weaved mats knee deep so as to show her legs with its whitish colour to the people who are the sole judge of the ceremony. Her arms and neck will be shown also. The days of wearing long *vala* and long sleeves, and rubbing oil are ceased. She, after all these obediences to her mother, has thus won the maiden consent of the fine gentleman.

Protracted physical virility is traditionally associated with the Tongan chiefs of the past. Mumui, the sixth Tu'i Kanokupolu, successfully bestrode the pre-Christian days of the eighteenth century till he was over a hundred years old. He fathered his last child at the age of eighty.

One of the early Tongan ministers called Pauli Taumoepeau embarked upon matrimony for the third time when he was seventy. His relations protested, reminding him that he had children and grandchildren who would look after him and provide him with everything he needed.

"I know," the old minister is said to have replied with a nostalgic look in his eye, "that you can feed me and clothe me. But there is one thing you and the mission cannot give me and that is what I am looking for!"

It used to be—and still is for that matter—an honour for a girl to bear a child to a chief. There was no bashful waiting for the curling eyelash to catch the eye and interest of a high ranking male. Father took care of all the essential preliminaries.

"If," as it was told to me, "you were the best looking chief in a village and I had a ripe young daughter, I should not wait for you to come to woo her. I should creep silently into your hut one night and say 'A heavenly blessing indeed it would be for a gangrenous old man like me to have a fair young grandson. I have brought my daughter so that she may have the honour of bearing you a son.'

"I should then leave her alone in your care and sleep on the verandah outside the hut until the early hours of the morning. Then, as the fowls began to fly down from their roosts in the banana trees, I should creep back into the house and take my daughter quietly away so that none might know what had taken place."

The object was thus presumably attained in the course of time while the proprieties were safeguarded.

Domestic animals in Tonga also seemed to develop special

characteristics and urges. The indigenous bush fowl showed no awareness of laying seasons. About any eleven months of the year were the off season; while the brief period of production required a constant watch lest it be missed altogether. When she did develop positive urges, the Tongan fowl could never be tempted into a comfortable straw nest. Roadside grass, a pile of leaves in the undergrowth or even the cold face of the garage floor seemed to offer more attraction for the meditations of a mother-to-be. When activity did begin, it was a period of daily laying until up to a dozen eggs had been deposited in a remote nest; then plonk on the eggs sat mother hen, and that was the end of the breakfast drive from her for that year.

The male of the species was equally disconcerting. We had two: a jet-black Don Juan at first and a more sedate colleague in white later. Don Juan was a peripatetic lover and displayed no interest in the domestic opportunities available to him. Whenever he could, he was off at a brisk trot round the garage corner, past the cement water tank beside the house, over the front garden and through the hedge to join a rival establishment across the road. He did at least return at dusk, but we did not enthuse over his attentive philanderings elsewhere. In the end, these proved to be his downfall. He dashed impatiently through the hedge in a violent rain squall one day and was crushed beneath the wheel of a passing car. We nursed him beside the stove fire that night, but I returned from the office next day to an expired Don Juan and a tearful wife. He was honoured with burial in the front garden where a wooden cross marked his final resting place.

The next rooster was an offspring of his predecessor; but his incestuous relationships did not seem to bother him. The new master soon developed a gratifying sense of preference for home instead of away matches, his principal indiscretion being to blow out his lungs beneath my window at an uncivilised hour each morning. Together with his neighbours, he maintained a nocturnal schedule of first call at eleven p.m., second call at two-thirty a.m. and general chaos from three-thirty onwards. It could thus be said with complete truth and no great shame that one had come home with the cocks.

The white rooster had noteworthy if theatrical devotion to his charges. On the rare occasions when an egg made its appearance, he dropped all other activity and made off all sails set to congratulate his spouse. This he did by joining in the chorus with a throaty baritone cackle and for a good five minutes the two of them hovered near the nest proclaiming their success. Following, I suppose, the basic magnetic law that unlike poles attract, his favourite was a little black hen, who stammered when she cackled. Her double-barrelled action suggested either that two hens had combined to produce one egg or, alternatively, that one hen had produced two eggs at the same time. Since neither was the case, the racket produced by the stammering hen and the white rooster was unwarrantably ostentatious.

If ceremonials are the framework of Tongan society, music, song and dance are the flesh and blood that bring all Polynesians pulsatingly alive. Although present-day Tongan singing has been influenced by Sankey and Moody and the dances are less uninhibited than those of the Cook Islands or Tahiti, the best Tongan singing is remarkably sonorous and the finest dancing exciting and graceful.

One of the oldest Tongan instruments is the bamboo nose flute. There is no sound quite like it: plaintive, yet penetrating like the piccolo in a symphony orchestra; but unlike the piccolo, its sound is soft and mellow. Queen Elizabeth and the Duke of Edinburgh were awakened by four nose flute players when they stayed their solitary night in Queen Salote's Palace. The instrument is believed to date back to the time of the first Tu'i Tonga in the twelfth century. The flute is closed at both ends and it is possible to blow it from either. There are six holes in each flute, five on one side and one directly below the third of the five holes. Only one note can be sounded at a time although it is common for several flutes to play together. The thumb of the left hand is used to stop the nostril which is not blowing the flute.

Playing the nose flute is now a dying art and the visitor to Tonga is more likely to see the Polynesian counterpart of the Trinidad steel drum. This is a large biscuit tin pounded by a fiercely irrepressible drummer who beats it first into submission and then, sometimes, into pulp. The toneless ear-splitting beat never fails to stimulate rhythmic response from the dancers.

No important celebration passes without dancing and song. Queen Salote had a discerning eye for a good dancer and the Palace troupe was accordingly the most skilful in Tonga. The dances vary in nature and origin. Some are solos or for small groups; others are for massed performance.

One of the older dances is the *me'etu'upaki*. This is a traditional religious dance, the *lali* being played in the early days by the Tu'i Tonga himself. As the dancers are elderly men, the movements are slow and unvaried. The music is chanted in two parts, but the meaning of the words has been lost. It is not contrapuntal and is rather monotonous. A few voices maintain one note while the others sing such melody as there is. Throughout the dance, each of the participants holds a light wooden instrument carved in the shape of a paddle.

Then there is the *'otuhaka*, the dance of the maidens of high rank. This is a sitting dance, the head, eyes, arms, fingers, nose and even the toes of the dancers all having their part and meaning. The precision of the gestures is extraordinary. The dance begins with a long drum solo after about thirty bars of which a silent, unaccompanied gesture dance begins. Then the dancers begin to sing in rough canon form in two parts. The rhythm becomes a little faster and the story more intriguing. Each twist of the finger or a twinkling of an eye has meaning and is often, as in other dances of Polynesia, a challenge to a warrior. Towards the end, as Thomson puts it, there is a sudden quickening with a long-drawn note or groan and dropping of the voice down the scale like an organ when the bellows give out.

The music of the *'otuhaka*, though still chanted, is more melodious than that of the *me'etu'upaki*. Another more modern sitting dance—the *ma'ulu'ulu*—was performed for Queen Elizabeth and the Duke of Edinburgh. The music and words were written by Queen Salote herself.

The *tau'olunga* is a graceful solo dance in which other dancers may participate. Temperatures always rise when the female dancers are joined and their own dancing stimulated by a provocative male dancer.

The *lakalaka* is sometimes loosely used to describe all Tongan dances, but it is comparatively new in Tonga. It was evolved soon after the first schools were opened by the Wesleyan missionaries in the early part of the nineteenth century; and it has now taken the place of the older dances as a national and ceremonial dance. The movements of other Polynesian dances have been incorporated into it. Both male and female singers and dancers assemble in one or more long rows. While the men dance, the women move their heads and arms without changing position. The melody is more consistent and since no drum is used the rhythm is less marked. The modern *lakalaka* is often written to celebrate special occasions; and the composers hold a place in Tongan life akin to that of the Trinidad calypsonian. They are composer, poet and dancing master in one. Important village events, visits by overseas dignitaries, the results of cricket or football matches, weddings, deaths and other events are all perpetuated in the words and music of the best-known of Tongan dances.

Tongan choirs are magnificent. Centred on the church, they form the basis of congregational singing of a quality not otherwise found outside Wales. I remember BBC commentator Wynford Vaughan Thomas, his eyes dimmed, as he listened to the rich sonorous sound of Prince Tungi's Maopa Choir as its hundred members sang the "Hallelujah Chorus" to him. Tungi inherited his deep musical interest from his mother. He used to import the scores of Bach, Mozart and Handel for his choir to learn; and he then transposed the orchestral parts for the brass band that played with his choir. All the choirs had self-taught conductors, few of whom had ever left the reef-girt islands in which they had been born. And yet they attempted, with resounding success, the masses of Mozart and the oratorios of Handel. The Queen and the Duke of Edinburgh listened enthralled to five hundred hand-picked Tongan voices, with the Maopa Band, singing the "Sanctus" from the Bach Mass in B Minor. And outside—the coconut palms, the thatched round-ended houses, the cries of the seabirds diving for fish on the reef, the grass skirts, the white beaches. Yet they would not be out of place in the Albert Hall.

The Christmas period is one of great musical activity and importance. The midnight services on Christmas Eve bring to an end the high jinks and fun that marks the day before Christmas everywhere; and throughout the rest of the day the churches are full. Presents are exchanged; a dozen loaves of bread, a can of kerosene, lamps, Tongan oil made from coconuts and herbs, mats, grass skirts and rolls of *tapa* cloth prepared from the bark of the *hiapo* tree, beaten flat and printed with earth and other dyes into colourful patterns.

There is Christmas dinner too. The family gathers round roast pig instead of turkey; and a doughy sweet made from breadfruit in a syrup sauce which takes the place of plum pudding. Pineapples, watermelons, fish, crabs, lobster, all jostle together before the feasting families. The houses are decorated with coconut palm leaves and flowers. Dancing and singing the songs of ancient Polynesia go on round the *kava* bowl far into the Christmas night. Even here, hangovers are not unknown.

The village bands come into their own as Christmas approaches. From about the beginning of December, the bands parade the villages and the streets of the towns, blowing their hearts out and having wonderful fun. A few days before our first Tongan Christmas, we were sitting down to dinner when I heard signs of subdued activity on the lawn outside the house. A minute later there was a lusty burst of blowing as thirty brown bandsmen treated us to their version of "Jingle Bells". They were collecting for a new mission building and were the first of many visitors we were to have. The conventional carol singers of other lands don't exist, but there are numerous little groups doing much the same thing with a couple of mouth-organs and their guitars. You can expect these minstrels at any time after dark and they are remarkably good at creeping silently and barefooted on to your front verandah before launching into melody. They are competent music-makers, and so they should be: they have to pass the strong arm of the law before they can begin their rounds. Every afternoon the Minister of Police held a personal audition of each group outside his office on the green lawns by the foreshore at Nuku'alofa. If they passed muster, they got a sealed permit and set off on the Christmas round; but the downcast eyes of some revealed that in their case the Minister had required them to withhold their musical talents from the public ear until the next Christmas festivity.

10 Three Thousand Virgins-And Me

HA'APAI lies to the north of Tongatapu. The main island is Lifuka, one of many that lie in straggling profusion about one hundred miles from Nuku'alofa. Their languid coconut palms and the brilliance of their iridescent beaches and lagoons give out a visual mesmerism all their own. Here in the inner heart of Polynesia are the South Sea paradise islands of the romanticist of past and present. Their maze-like reefs are intractable hazards for the unwary navigator; but their unspoilt charm is reward in full for those sturdy enough to venture among them by cutter or ketch. The Tongans of Ha'apai are of a world that is past; and their special character is as distinct today as it was 200 years ago—notwithstanding the intrusion of modern bureaucracy in the shape of a Governor, a post office, a telegraph station and the official gazette. Queen Salote always looked upon Ha'apai as "home"; here she was at peace with her people.

The *Hifofua* landed me at Lifuka about twenty-four hours after we had sailed from Nuku'alofa. The Government wooden ketch, she was, at that time, ponderous, uncertain and battle-scarred. I shall not forget the spectacle of a hitherto dignified Australian Judge of Her Tongan Majesty's Supreme Court wrapped in mortifying agony round the stern rail but ten minutes after we had slackened the jetty hawsers. You had to be sturdy of heart and stomach to face the unpacific Pacific in the bosom of the *Hifofua*.

The voyages of the ancient Polynesian come vividly alive as miracles of human endurance at such times. I suspect that they do as well to the present-day Tongan, for unexpectedly there seems little difference between their susceptibility to seasickness in rough weather and our own. The wonder of it is not merely that the ancients arrived more or less intact at the other end, but that they then not infrequently contrived to embark on successful campaigns of pillage and warfare before sailing homewards. Whether the hazards of the journey rested more in physical than in oceanic violence, the gaps in the ranks of the returning warriors were there nonetheless; and even today the departure of a cutter to Tongatapu or Vava'u brings forth the entire population to shout and weep at the beach with a profusion of feeling that still reflects the days when no sweetness lay in the sadness of such parting, for there was no certainty of return.

Clad in unrelieved black mourning for a deceased relative, barefooted and wearing the customary *ta'ovala*, the Governor stood in solitary state at the edge of the tiny wharf as we arrived. Fifteen yards behind were the people of Pangai, the main village—men, women, children and babies, clasped firmly in the ample arms of eight policemen and all in a fever of restless, but silent impatience for their seventy-odd returning kinsmen travelling as deck passengers on the *Hifofua*. Governor Fielakepa shook hands with the left hand; some years before, he had suffered the misfortune of semi-paralysis in his right side. Moving with difficulty, heavy and ponderous of manner and body, Fielakepa did not find that his responsibilities weighed lightly on him. He dropped dead, suddenly, in September 1956, just before a meeting of the Privy Council at the Palace in Nuku'alofa. He was blessed with a patient and gentle wife and he himself could refuse no man a request properly put to him.

From the wharf, we walked to the Governor's residence, fifty yards from the end of the jetty and resting cosily in the coconut palms. It was nine a.m. I was due to inspect Government offices and interview the staff; but the significant cracking of stones on the *kava* root meant that the appointed hour of official visitation would as usual be a bad second to the pleasurable procrastinations of Tongan courtesies. The *kava* was well-matured and had a refreshing tang like that of Fijian kava. And when the bowl was at last empty, I thought I could now get down to the business of the visit.

I might have known otherwise. The truck which was to take us to the hospital, the gaol and the new causeway which was Fielakepa's pride and joy, was due at ten o'clock. When, after no apparent effort to hasten its arrival, it finally arrived two hours late, neither Fielakepa nor the driver betrayed concern for the delay. "*Tuku'aipe*" is the Tongan counterpart of the Arabic "*ma'lish*" and the magniloquent Gallic shrug which disclaims all responsibility for the calamitous acts of god or man.

"*Tuku'aipe*," they said and "*Tuku'aipe*" I replied. Anyhow the driver of the truck had three chins, a disarmingly oleaginous laugh and two hundred and fifty pounds avoirdupois. He rejoiced in the name of *Pinati* (or Peanut), and who could be cross with a giant with a name like that?

Fielakepa, I found, was soon exhausted by our labours and at three o'clock he began to show increasing signs of restlessness. We returned to his house where he sat immobile for the next two hours fondling his "saucepan special" battery radio. The content of the broadcasts appeared to be unimportant. The tuning was always slightly off centre and the volume sufficient to raise the scalp off my head.

In the evening, the local belles put on a dance in the house of the district manager of the Copra Board. Guitars and voices in harmony clanged away with enormous zest and I gave a prize for the best *tau'olunga*. Shortly after midnight, I returned to the Governor's residence to find him seated crosslegged on the verandah with a dozen or so of his attendants and an amply filled *kava* bowl in the corner. No invitation was necessary and I joined them. We talked till two about the glorious past of Tonga, its politics and religion, its royal wars and royal romances. Then Fielakepa who had not spoken for some time, called for silence from the reclining figures nearby.

"The *Sekelitali*," he said, "has been with us in Tonga for over a year. He has worked for our Queen and our people during the visit to these islands of his Queen and her husband. And we have seen today a copy of the book in our tongue which he has written about the Royal Visit. I have accordingly considered that the time has now come to bestow upon him a chiefly Tongan name."

"*Koia, mo'oni*," echoed the shadows, "what you say is indeed true."

"Then, *Sekelitali*," said Fielakepa, as he turned to me, "I hereby name you 'Toluafe', the title of the great navigator of the old Tu'i Tonga and that which Tuita the head of the Queen's navigators also bears.

And Tuita, one of Her Majesty's Nobles, who was seated beside the Governor nodded his assent.

"I am," I responded, "deeply grateful, but I hope that I shall not be called upon to justify my qualifications for the appointment."

In the course of Polynesian time, I returned to Nuku'alofa, and there began to enquire about the illustrious Tongan whose mantle had so unexpectedly fallen on to my shoulders. The story revealed itself in this wise.

In the seventeenth century there lived a chief called Tuita who was renowned throughout the land for his skill in seamanship and navigation. Tuita often ventured as far afield as Fiji, Samoa and the Wallis Islands. On these occasions he used the *kalia* or large double canoe, the bridge across which was a hut about the size of an average living room today. He had a crew of thirty and frequently carried about a hundred passengers.

Towards the end of a long and vigorous life—he is believed to have lived till he was well over ninety—Tuita accompanied his King on a journey to Fiji. The royal navigators, 'Aku'ola and Ula, were also the captains of the King's canoe, while Tuita, who was by this time completely blind, sailed with his son in a second canoe. On the way back from Viti Levu, the royal flotilla ran into the heavy south-east storms of the season and for ten days no land was sighted. When the weather again grew calm, the King invited his navigators to tell him where they were. Reluctantly and with shame, they confessed that they did not know; for the severity of the winds had been such that even they, the wisest and most skilled of the King's navigators, could not tell whither they should row.

Much angered by their incompetence, the King called for Tuita's canoe to draw near so that the old navigator's opinion could be sought as to how far they had progressed towards Tonga. Tuita told one of his attendants to carry him to the side of the canoe so that he could reach out and touch the water passing by. When he had done so, Tuita said to those who watched, "We are not yet near Tonga for these are the ocean waters of Fiji."

And when they asked, "But how can you know?" he replied, "I can tell by the feel of the sea."

So Tuita pointed the way ahead and the canoes sailed on as he directed. When the day was spent, he asked his son to describe the appearance of the tropic stars and after he had heard enough, he again gave instructions for their course.

Next morning Tuita asked his son to splash the sea in his face. As he felt the texture of the water, he said, "This is a Lakemba wave. Soon you will see the Fiji island of Lakemba which is nearly half way on our journey to Tonga." And so it was that in the afternoon, the palm trees of Lakemba grew out of the sea ahead, just as the blind navigator had promised.

When the King saw the island, he called Tuita's canoe and said to 'Aku'ola and Ula: "You are the heads of my navigators, but you are the sleeping heads with eyes which do not see. From this time henceforth, the blind Tuita shall be my chief navigator."

So they made their way safely on to Tonga, and to this day, Tuita is the head of the royal navigators . . .

The original Tuita had, however, another claim to fame which has given him a special place in the Tongan fantasy of the past. In the long days of his physical virility, Tuita was renowned as a great seafaring lover.

After every virginal conquest, it was his practice to tie a knot in the long *kafa* or sinnet cord he wore round his *ta'ovala*. Married women and unmarried girls no longer in their original state of virtuous innocence were not excluded from romantic investigation, but did not qualify for record in the *kafa*. The crew of Tuita's canoe knew well what the knots in his *kafa* meant, so that when he died not many months after his honourable recognition by the King, they made haste to examine the testimony of his prowess in the art of lovemaking. They found that the *kafa* was nearly 200 yards long and that it contained exactly 3,000 knots, of which none had been tied twice.

When the chiefly successor to the title of Tuita was appointed, he too was named "Toluafe" meaning "three thousand" and this custom has been handed down to the present day.

Life being what it now is, the present Tuita has perforce to be content with the shadow and not the substance of what is implicit in his second and more picturesque title.

And, likewise, Margaret tells me, must I.

11 Democracy at Work

WHOEVER said "Truth is absolute" can't have spent any time in the Friendly Islands. The Tongan is a skilled exponent of the art of evasive responses. Domestic and social diplomacy is a highly developed feature of his art of living. He is also a manipulator of words—words the unequivocal meaning of which was not previously in issue. The man of rank may find it hard to get at the whole truth. The reason is that the commoner tells his chief what he thinks the chief wishes to know or would like to hear. Unpalatable tidings are guarded from his ears.

Tongan society flourishes on a condoned freedom to mix near-truth with mild inaccuracy. It goes something like this. The grass has all been cut, when the knives haven't yet been reclaimed from the last person who took, borrowed or stole them; the new copra has been dried and weighed, when the overseer has in fact made off with the receipts from last week's labour in order to pay for his daughter's wedding; and, yes, Sir, the letter has been delivered—when actually it still awaits the return of the messenger from his last errand.

It is not unlike the *dhobi* I knew in Palestine who was always bringing my laundry *bukra* which meant "tomorrow". Or at least it meant "tomorrow" until tomorrow came. I then discovered that it meant the day after this one or the day after that . . .

So it was one evening that I said to my medical friend Posesi who plays cricket and ought to know better at his age: "Posesi, when are we going to play cricket at Pea Village again."

"I think," replies Posesi, "very soon."

I am unimpressed, knowing by now his temporising ways. And we talk about other less important matters.

Next morning my telephone rings and Posesi, fired with unusual vigour, announces that the Pea people are waiting for me to come that afternoon. Gratified by his thoughtfulness and prepared to believe, I drive off to Pea where I find one sick old man and a pig.

"Where," I ask, "are my cricketers?"

"Oh," he replies, "Posesi sent a message half an hour ago that you wanted to come and play cricket this afternoon, but all the young men are away at our gardens planting the new season's yams. It was too late to bring them back."

The first Tongan phrase to make its mark on the newcomer is *mahalo pe*. If translatable at all, this means "maybe", or "perhaps". More refined variations include "maybe yes", "maybe no", or "I don't really know, but I'm certainly not going to admit it." The effect is irresistible, said, as it always is, through pearly teeth and a disarming smile. Life anyway is not contained in a strait-jacket, to be bound in words and imprisoned in the chill darkness of logic. It is rich and lustful and alive with the warmth of a sun which boils the blood and titillates the brain.

The Tongan has not yet learned the truth about time. It has no vital meaning for him. "They can cope with almost anything else," said a despairing New Zealand hospital matron one day, "but they just have trouble with time."

"How come, you say? Time's easy; time's ten o'clock and on my hands and an American news magazine and an experiment with. Time's easy." Well, if that's what you think, so did we until we learned otherwise—in the Friendly Islands.

Shortly after we arrived in Nuku'alofa, we held a cocktail party which was to begin at six o'clock. At least we thought we were going to have it at six o'clock, but the first guests—a local dignitary and his wife—arrived forty minutes early when we were still in the bath. The other guests turned up between then and twenty minutes to six. The last to arrive were the host and hostess who put in a harassed appearance at ten to six.

"Ah," we said, "Put that down to experience. In Tonga the guests are obviously supposed to be all there and the party half over by the time you invite people for. We'll know next time."

Then we went to a large feast. Two hundred guests. Invitation

Buying whale meat

The whale boat brings in the remains of the carcase

Queen Salote with Vilai Tupou, her ADC and half-brother, in 1945

time one p.m. We duly arrived at twelve-thirty and found a disconcerted host roasting pigs in an earth oven. No one else turned up till one-twenty.

A month later an important chiefly feast, which the Queen was to attend. We tried again and turned up on the dot to find Her Majesty installed and 300 guests making impressive inroads into vast quantities of earth-baked pork and chicken. The time had been changed but we had not been told.

"Anyway," said Margaret, when I complained, "have you tried cooking for eight, let alone 300, and getting it all ready on time?"

At the end of 1954, the Tongan Civil Service structure underwent a belated overhaul and salaries review. The Commissioner and I went north to Ha'apai and Vava'u to see conditions and interview civil servants in the two other main island groups. In Ha'apai, we were entertained by the Governor to a modest little feast on the sands of the shore where Captain Cook first named Tonga the Friendly Islands in 1773. We sailed away six hours after our arrival amid one of those demonstrative and tearful Polynesian farewells which still express the fears of a sentimental people for whom, two hundred years ago, a journey across the sea was a voyage into the unknown and goodbye might be forever. When we drew away from the little jetty, the tearful damsels restored the joys of life by plunging one after the other off the end of the wharf into the sea; and, in a moment, were shrieking with the zestful laughter of the sunshine at the bawdy comments of their deserted swains above.

All this made no impression on the ex-naval petty officer who was captain of the Tonga Copra Board's auxiliary ketch on which we were travelling. "Those cunning clerks," he fumed, "have gathered up all the pretty girls in Ha'apai to come down and weep for more money. Know what they're about, those chaps." Which, we thought, was a little ungracious after "those chaps" had given him such a succulently cooked lunch.

At Vava'u, we returned to a more sophisticated world where the *Tofua* calls each month and where internal comings and goings are of less consequence. Here the more ostentatious Vava'uan had full play. We were entertained to a lavish feast, attended by half the populace, followed by a succession of emotionally charged pleas for salary increases by and on behalf of our impoverished Civil Service hosts. In the evening there was a Grand Ball in the courthouse with ceremonial introductions, floor shows and guitars, dancing girls and warm beer. Village maidens, dressed in their best, clutched each other in mutual support along the sides of the hall. The Vava'u Civil Service was proving itself well worthy of such an historic visitation, although the Governor repeatedly emphasised that he greatly regretted the poverty-stricken inadequacy of the welcome; but, well, he said, you know how it is . . .

Next day was Sunday and the Governor invited us to attend the special Wesleyan service to commemorate the birth of King George Tupou I. We duly reached the church at eight-forty a.m., five minutes before the appointed hour for the service to begin. The only soul in sight was an apparently permanent occupant dozing in a corner. He knew of no arrangement for a service, but as that in itself wasn't anything unusual, I laid little store by it. We waited for ten minutes and then left in some perplexity. At half past nine we decided to try again and returned to find a mildly apologetic Governor awaiting us and the service about to begin. In response to our unspoken question, he said that the bell-ringer was late and, anyway, no one ever goes to church till they hear the bell ringing, do they?

"No," I reflected sadly, "I suppose they don't. But you did say last night . . ."

And then I stopped. What was the use? They just have trouble with time.

The curious thing is that the elected members of the Tongan Legislative Assembly—more worldly-wise souls perhaps—didn't seem to have any such bother with the clock. They sat from ten to twelve in the forenoon; and from two to four in the afternoon. If the referee's whistle for the start of the day's play was sometimes a little late, the morning and afternoon closure never was. At two minutes to twelve or four, a restiveness came over the House. A speaker lost in oratory was soon made aware of it, as the other members rapped on the tables and stamped their feet when the clock showed time. And out they trooped into the sunshine.

"Maybe," I said, when I saw this on the first occasion, "there is more in this time business than I thought." But I never did get to the bottom of it—except that the legislators could not be persuaded to go over to an annual, as distinct from a daily, parliamentary allowance.

The report of the Salaries Commissioner was duly published. The Civil Service gave it the cool reception reserved for such documents and it received the usual opposition from the legislative opponents of the Government. After the report had been examined administratively, it went to the Privy Council. It was adopted as Government policy and then presented to the Legislative Assembly for debate on a motion proposing its acceptance and the voting of the funds necessary to carry out its recommendations.

The Commissioner had made a thorough appraisal of the Tongan Civil Service structure and his recommendations were interdependent. Amendments to one or two grades or posts would have upset the lot and set off a chain reaction. It was important that this should be avoided, but there was a danger of special pleading during the debate. As Tungi was away and the Commissioner had left the Kingdom, the Deputy Premier thought that I might meet Legislative Assembly members informally to explain the detailed recommendations in the Report and to answer questions about it. We believed that this would reduce the possibility of personal jobbery.

We were wrong. A letter had been sent by the Deputy Premier to all members proposing that I should meet with them in a few days and that the House should adjourn for this purpose. On the following morning, the Representatives of the People were steaming with indignation; and I again found myself, unwittingly, on the legislative pillory. A breach of the Constitution was, they said, imminent.

Tu'akoi: Mr. Speaker and Members of the House, I would like to refer to a letter which was handed to us yesterday afternoon in which the Deputy Premier suggested that the House adjourn after twelve noon next Monday in order that a special meeting of members be held in the afternoon which is to be attended by the Secretary to the Government for a discussion of the Report by the Salaries Revision Commissioner. I ask for the opinion of you, Mr. Speaker, and members as to whether the suggestion is not objectionable to anyone's view; whether you would be satisfied with it since it is now nearly two centuries and nothing like it had ever been attempted. I fear that this attempt to bring the Secretary to the House may develop into making him a permanent member. The House should not accept this suggestion. Mr. Speaker, the Secretary should be informed that if he has any advice to offer to give it to the Premier. If the House is adjourned and the Secretary allowed to come in it would mean a breach of the Constitution. Tonga has recently been advised that no European should be allowed to enter any of the high councils of the land but the Treasurer has been allowed to be a member of the House. This is another attempt to bring in another European. Mr. Speaker, if this suggestion is approved by the House, I ask that individual members be not bound to attend.

Governor of Ha'apai: Mr. Speaker, he is coming just to answer questions. He will only answer any questions put to him. He will not be voting. He will be here to make things clear and nothing else.

Tu'akoi: He will not take part in the balloting, but he will take part in the debate.

Tuita: The Governor has not read his law well. Honourable Members, what advice could this officer offer you when you are here to deliberate independently? This is unlawful. I support the Second Member for Tongatapu that the Secretary be not allowed to come to the House. Stop him from coming here and instruct him to attend to his office duties.

Governor of Ha'apai: Honourable Member for the Nobles, is the public debarred from the House?

Tuita: Spectators are not debarred like those at the back there. They could come and hear but not to take part in the business of the House.

Governor of Ha'apai: No one is debarred from coming to the House.

Tu'akoi: Mr. Speaker, may I clarify the issue. The letter asked for a special meeting of members and the Secretary to the Government. He is coming for a meeting with us which would be different to the presence here of spectators. The spectators are voiceless, but he is coming to influence us.

Minister of Police: Mr. Speaker, he is coming for a special meeting with us so that we could ask him questions. He is coming so that we could ask him anything which is not clear to us and he would advise and leave; then we would proceed with our deliberations.

Tu'akoi: Mr. Speaker, is this proposed meeting part of the official business of the House? If it is to be an independent meeting then I would like to address the House.

Speaker: It will be part of the work of the House. It is to clarify certain parts of the work of the House.

Tu'akoi: Mr. Speaker, the Constitution provides that the House should comprise the Ministers, seven Representatives of the People and seven Representatives of the Nobles. It also provides for the free admission of the public to the House as spectators; they are not allowed to speak. If officers have been allowed to the House in the past in the manner in which it is proposed that the Secretary should be admitted it was wrong. The proper thing to do is to ask the officer to submit what he has to submit to the House in writing.

This proposal would be against the Constitution and the law. I ask, Mr. Speaker, that the attendance at this proposed meeting to which the Secretary will be called should not be made compulsory. What purpose would be served in his coming? The report is not his work. I object to any discussion with the Secretary in Her Majesty's Legislative Assembly.

Afuha'amango: Mr. Speaker, ever since I received this letter yesterday I have been trying to recall whether the House had any dispute over the Report to warrant the introduction of outside advice. I do not remember the House having any dispute over the report. Mr. Speaker, this is an unusual thing. There is something big behind this, Mr. Speaker. Why should an outside person be procured to advise you, Mr. Speaker. There is a spy who initiated this move. This thing is dirty.

Tuakihekolo: Mr. Speaker and Hon. Members, I have no misgivings regarding this matter. There are parts of the Report which are not too clear to me, so I think this would offer an opportunity to have these cleared up. The Secretary is not coming to participate in the business of the House. He is coming for a special meeting with members. I am not an expert in financial matters and I would welcome this opportunity to get from the Secretary any knowledge which might assist me when the Report is considered. The Secretary is not going to persuade the House. Moreover, this officer has been suspected of having more to do with the Report than what appeared on the surface, and this would be an opportunity to interrogate him in that regard. Therefore, I have no fears concerning this proposed meeting.

Tuita: I am not afraid, but I suggest that this officer should attend his own work. I, myself, know very little about finance, but what has this officer to offer us by way of advice? We have the Minister of Finance here to advise us. The Secretary should attend to his own work. I object to his coming here and leaving his office work undone.

Minister of Police: Mr. Speaker, the issue is now clear. I consider that this will give members an opportunity to question the Secretary. The Ministers are not in a position to give members what they may want to know about the Report. The Secretary was the officer who was closest to the Salaries Commissioner. If members think that the Report is clear then all I can say is that Ministers will not be able to answer any questions which you may wish to ask.

Tu'akoi: Mr. Speaker, may I put a question to the Hon. Minister of Police? Mr. Minister, did you approve the Report in Privy Council?

Minister of Police: Yes.

Tu'akoi: Then you ought to know something about the Report and be able to answer any questions made in connection with the Report.

Minister of Police: Do you mean to suggest that I should be fully conversant with every aspect of the Report?

Tu'akoi: And do you say that you are not prepared to answer any question put to you?

Minister of Police: I will if permitted by the Speaker, but I am free to say what I would like to say.

Afuha'amango: Mr. Minister, do you mean to say that you are free to tell lies to the House?

Minister of Police: Have you ever known me to have told the House anything untruthful? You have been guilty of a grave misbehaviour yourself when you said "swine" in the House the other day.

Afuha'amango: Mr. Speaker, the Minister is swearing at me, when he is referring to swine.

Minister of Police: Had you known the meaning of the word "swine" you would never have used it. As this particular member will be the one who will have the most questions to ask about the Report, he should be thankful for the opportunity of having the Secretary to answer his questions. Therefore let us take a vote on it.

Afeaki: It is immaterial to me whether the Secretary attends the meeting or not, but I assure you that it will take at least two weeks to ask and answer queries arising out of the Report. It will certainly take more than two hours, for there are many matters in the Report that conflict. This will afford an opportunity to get these matters cleared up, for I am sure that there will be quite a prolonged discussion on the Report.

Speaker: The question is now quite clear, and we should now take a vote on it.

Tuita: Mr. Speaker, may I ask the Minister of Finance a question? If he gives me a satisfactory reply then I will change my mind. Is the Secretary to Government the author of a book?

Treasurer: Yes, he did write a book.

Tuita: Then I would agree to his attending the meeting.

Speaker: Those in favour that the Secretary to Government be allowed to attend the meeting next Monday afternoon as requested by the Deputy Premier in order to advise the members on the Salaries Revision Report, kindly raise your hands.

Clerk: 13—6. Motion carried.

So the meeting was held. A genial and friendly mood prevailed. The Report was debated in the House and went through virtually unscathed. The emotional energy of the Opposition had already been spent.

12 Sipoti Fakatonga—Sport in the Tongan Way

LIKE the Fijian, the Tongan seems to start an unfamiliar sport with inborn advantages. He readily grasps the main ingredients—although not perhaps the finer tactical points—of tennis, rugby, cricket, roller skating, golf, badminton, with enviable ease. This is possible because of a quick and faultless eye matched by powerful wrists and legs. You see this in tennis where a Tongan style of play has been adopted to suit his talents. Long raking backline shots or lobs are not for him. In doubles play, opposing pairs rapidly close to the net and full volleys rattle back and forth with bewildering speed. It almost seems a mark of weakness to let the ball touch the ground.

The lively interest with which rugby football is followed in Tonga was stimulated during our stay by a tour of an Australian team. The visitors were, it was said, of roughly the standard of a good Sydney first-grade XV. Five matches were played, including two "tests", of which the Australians won one—their only victory. If, from the result card, the Australians were not conspicuously successful, in every other way they were outstandingly so. The Tongan is quick to respond to cleanliness and sportsmanship in opponents; and as the visitors' captain remarked in his farewell speech, on not one occasion in five matches did the whistle blow for foul play.

Transported overnight from the bustle and hurly-burly of their cities, the Australians found the relaxed and easy-going atmosphere of Nuku'alofa enchantingly seductive from the moment of their arrival. The tropic nights glowed with singing, dancing and feasting, with Tonga's seemingly inexhaustible supply of roast sucking pig the staple item in an exotic and luxuriant diet.

In the procedure for the games, the Australians found unexpected local differences. At club matches, chiefs are usually present. Before play begins, the two teams parade down the field and then—in drilled unison—bow before the chiefly personages. Public acknowledgment of rank and nobility once paid, the game proceeds. At the end of the match, the teams march side by side off the field to the same spot, where the performance is repeated.

With their valedictory obeisances rewarded by a formal round of applause, the teams return again to the centre of the field where they proceed to cheer each other, the referee, the linesmen and frequently, if they have appeared to enjoy themselves, the chiefs as well. After all that, the battle really is over and reluctantly the participants make way for the next teams to perform their preliminary formalities. Duly apprised of this custom, the Australians carried it out in all their matches to the gratified pleasure of their Tongan hosts.

For the first "test" match, Queen Salote, her two Royal sons, the British Agent and Consul, and the Ministers of the Cabinet were present with their wives. The Tongan pulls out all the stops on such occasions. He is proud of the numerous brass bands which pound away in schools, colleges and villages to the detriment, at times, it has been suggested, of other perhaps more essential activities. One of the best bands is that of Tonga College which was in attendance on this occasion and determined to do its stuff—as events were to show—to the end.

After the Royal Family had taken their seats, the British Agent and Consul arrived and the band played the first half of the British National Anthem. A few minutes later the Queen alighted from her car, the crowds arose for their own National Anthem, the Tongan flag was lowered by a massive police sergeant and the Royal Standard hoisted to join the Australian flag on twin flagpoles above the royal enclosure. The band struck up the "Invercargill March" and side by side, Australian green and Tongan red marched across the ground. After the usual preliminaries, the members of both teams were presented to Queen Salote, a truly regal figure as she stood to greet them and to welcome the visitors to her kingdom. As they were presented, each member of the Tongan team bent his knee and kissed his Queen's hand.

Meanwhile, the band had been tacking up and down the field and was only persuaded to retreat to its enclosure when the crowd made it evident that it had come to watch football and not to listen to interminable marches. And so the game began, the irrepressible enthusiasm of the bandmaster being such, however, that his musicians burst into a rollicking "Colonel Bogey" at the precise moment that Tonga kicked off.

After weeks of sunshine the ground was like iron and for more than half the game there was a clear sky and a light breeze. Then, as is so often the case in these Polynesian islands, the unexpected happened. A menacing grey cloud invaded the blue, grew in size until it enveloped the whole sky and five minutes later burst in fury upon the ground.

Soon the field was a lake dotted with little brown patches. The match became a mud scramble and both referee and players gave up hope of doing much else but serve their sentence. In the absence of anything now resembling football, there was one notable consolation. With the advent of the rain, the bandmaster found his second wind and lashed his saturated musicians with an enthusiasm remarkable as the only thing by then undampened. For nearly thirty minutes the band played without pause, although musically-minded listeners observed that the first tuba player had developed an unusual warble.

Over five inches of rain fell that afternoon and evening. Somehow the game struggled to an Australian victory by eight points to six. The formalities were performed with laudable devotion and we retreated homewards, my new Panama devastated beyond revival. As we left, the bandsmen with water over their bare ankles, their music sheets floating in a pulpy mass, and their limbs and instruments streaming with chill rain, were making a last go of it.

The Kolofo'ou Rugby Football Club put on a dance that evening for the Australians. The Queen's second son, Prince Fatafehi Tu'ipelehake, and his wife, Princess Melenaite, were present and during the evening the guests were entertained with some Tongan dances. I was standing with Melenaite a few yards from their table as we watched the performance. She accepted a cigarette which I offered but refused the match which followed. I asked her why and she leant forward and whispered "I can't smoke standing up when Fatafehi is sitting down." I moved away and returned a few minutes later to find Melenaite happily smoking her cigarette. In answer to my raised eyebrow, she replied with a twinkle in her eye, "It's all right now—he's standing up." And there indeed across the room was her husband no longer seated and engaged in conversation with the Judge. Melenaite had seized her opportunity and Tongan propriety was satisfied.

We had received an elegantly printed invitation to the dance from "the President, His Royal Highness Prince 'Uluvalu and the members of the Kolofo'ou Football Club." The President was not, however, in attendance to receive or to preside at the entertainment of his guests. When we took our leave of Prince Tu'ipelehake, we asked him to extend our thanks to the absent President for his kindness in inviting us to his dance. He said he would—next morning, because the royal president was at home in bed, asleep. No, he was not ill. It was just that the hour was a little advanced and the occasion perhaps a little too formal for him to be able to carry out his presidential functions in the manner appropriate to the post. He was Tu'ipelehake's son and he was but five years old.

Deserting the game of rugby football for one day, the Australians played a cricket match. On the face of it, their opponents did not appear unduly formidable—the men of Pea village—whose cricket is played on a concrete pitch laid on the only level strip of earth in the middle of the village. Over a century ago their land was the scene of some of the bloodiest fighting which culminated in the ascendancy of King George Tupou I and the acceptance of Christianity throughout Tonga. Pea was one of the last strongholds to hold out against King George and the villagers of today are proud of their historic resilience in adversity. The warrior of courage, Liemalohi, had come from Pea.

The fighting talent of the youth of the village is now expressed, among other ways, in the ferocity with which they sling a cricket ball down the concrete, the powerful nonchalance with which it is propelled by the batsman over the nearby palms and the unerring skill of the fieldsmen whose natural hazards include thatched houses, trees, piles of drying coconuts and holes.

One of the tricks of the fielding trade, as I learned to my cost, is to hide behind a house until the batsman has forgotten you and is lulled into thinking that a lusty pull to square leg will comfortably clear your shelter as a well-merited *ono* or six. You then dash out into the open, seize the ball from mid-air, and claim your victim, supported vociferously by the bowler. The village is then assured of a protracted and earthy controversy as to whether the catch should be allowed or not. Views about this usually work out at twelve all—each team has its own umpire—and the whole village is soon involved in a splendid display of oratory, with eye-witnesses for both prosecution and defence emerging from all sorts of unlikely places. Since the game has no time limit, such volatile councils of war proceed until a mutually acceptable solution is achieved when the game continues amid general merriment and goodwill.

Tongan umpires can also be disconcerting to cricketers from elsewhere. I bowled my first ball in Tonga with the umpire standing two feet away from the line of the stumps. Having, like all batsmen, suffered from inexplicable lbw decisions, I suggested to the umpire that he move closer to his proper place. He smiled politely and stayed where he was.

It occurred to me that he might make a visual adjustment before announcing a decision on an lbw appeal. This possibility was dispelled three balls later. The batsman played down the track to an in-swinger moving away outside the leg stump. He missed and the ball struck his forward pad knee-high. *Mate*, announced the umpire, meaning "dead" or in this case "out". I had made no appeal. I protested mildly and the batsman lingered in justifiable innocence. He was permitted to remain.

Meanwhile, the umpire, with an air of total concentration, remained planted at the on-side edge of the bowling crease. I asked the captain of the opposition, when he came in to bat, if anything could be done about this. He had been educated at Newington College in Sydney and we spoke the same cricket language.

He grinned. "Don't you know the reason why he won't stand behind the stumps?"

"No," I said, "tell me".

"Well, he's being polite to you. It would be discourteous of him to stand behind the stumps so close to you as you bowl. It is not our custom. And he got a bit rattled by his lbw mistake."

I remembered the Fijian team which once walked off the ground in a huff because their chief, who opened the batting, was bowled with the first ball of the match.

So we went on with the game. After a few overs, the umpire, having got used to me, I suppose, was persuaded to stand where he should. Later, as I waited to bat, there was what is generally described as a confident appeal for a catch behind the wicket. The other umpire's finger went up. I reached for my batting gloves and started out for the pitch. Someone said, "Where are you off to?"

The bowler was about to bowl again and the batsman had not budged. What, pray, was this?

"I thought he was out. The umpire certainly gave him out".

"Ah, but not in Tonga. When a Tongan umpire puts his finger up, he is saying to the batsman, 'that's all right. You can carry on. You're not out this time'."

And throughout the three years I played cricket in Tonga, the raised finger of a Tongan umpire invariably meant the opposite to what it does anywhere else.

There is, however, one Tongan cricketing habit which is even more disconcerting when first encountered. A cheer-leader is surreptitiously appointed by the fielding side. If the fieldsmen seem to be slacking off a bit or the batsmen are achieving too many *ono*, the cheer-leader shouts "*pasi*" in a warlike baritone. At this signal, every fieldsman leaps in the air and claps his hands two or three times, which is what the word means. Unfortunately, there does not seem to be any counter to this oral torment. It is a little hard on a batsman who may get *pasi* from slips, gully and point just as he is playing a nasty out-swinger.

All this, of course, ran true to form when, on a college field, the Australian openers faced their first Tongan bowler. It went on spasmodically through the innings and one retreating batsman summed it all up, "These jokers put the fear of hell into a chap," he said. "Not only do they bowl like demons but they all shout blue murder at you every now and again. Fair gives you the jitters, even though they seem to be smiling all the time."

And well might the Tongans smile, for their opponents were all out for 50 by lunch (Tongan style) and in the afternoon 168 was on the board for 3 wickets, before another deluge ended play for the day. Playing as a guest with Pea on this occasion I noticed that the Tongan scorer had wistfully headed the sheet "Pea Village v. Australia," which recalled Hugh de Selincourt's little fantasy *How our village beat the Australians.*

Regrettably, *these* were not *those* Australians, but it was an agreeable thought that I had played for the first, if assuredly the last, time against . . . Australia!

13 The Sabbath

THE preoccupations of the Friendly Island Sunday are church, food and slumber. There is ample measure of all three and little else. The Constitution declares that:

> The Sabbath Day shall be sacred in Tonga for ever and it shall not be lawful to do work or play games or trade on the Sabbath. And any agreement made or document witnessed on this day shall be counted void and shall not be recognised by the Government.

In addition, the statute book contains legislation known as the Order in Public Places Act. Like most of its kind, this sets out to establish a prohibition of liberties which many of us have at some time taken or have yearned to take. We may not ride, drive cattle or car carelessly, recklessly or furiously; we may not deposit dirt, rubbish, carrion or offal on any public way; we may not fly kites discharge any stone or other missile or set off fireworks; we may not shout or beat any drum, tin or tank without just cause (whatever that may be); we can call "sail-ho", but we may not permit our band to practise between ten at night and six in the morning; we must see to it that our children over six years of age are adequately clad; we must think twice before we erect a barbed wire fence facing any public way; we can only discharge our firearm with the permission of the mayor; and if we possess a stallion, we are required to ensure that he does not indulge in activity calculated to increase his kind within the boundaries of a town. All very inhibiting.

The observance of the Sabbath has, however, a special section all to itself:

> Whoever shall do any work on the Sabbath day such as house-

An aerial view of Nuku'alofa. The Palace and Royal Chapel are beside the foreshore towards the rear of the picture. The Free Wesleyan Church of Tonga is in the right foreground

Tuimalila, the ancient and battle-scarred Palace tortoise. Reputedly brought to Tonga by Captain Cook in the 1770s, he died after a long and noble life in the grounds of the Palace on the 19th May, 1966

Prince Tungi, now King Taufa'ahau Tupou IV (left), and his brother Prince Tu'ipelehake (right), their wives Princess Mata'aho and Princess Melenaite with the Governor of Fiji, Sir Derek Jakeway, and Lady Jakeway in 1964

The Palace at Nuku'alofa. The royal standard is at the masthead

> building boat-building gardening fishing or conveying any thing by boat or waggon except in cases of emergency and whoever shall discharge a firearm in the town or country or engage in any game such as cricket football lawn tennis golf bowls or similar games and dancing *lakalakas fa'ahiula* and such like pastimes shall be liable to a fine not exceeding five pounds or be imprisoned with hard labour for not more than three months in default of payment:
>
> Provided always that no proceedings shall be taken under this section in respect of anything done in accordance with the terms of a permit granted by Cabinet in case of emergency.

A party of American tourists fell victim of this law on one occasion. Having conveyed themselves to a nearby fishing ground on Sunday, they returned ashore in the late afternoon into the ample arms of the Nuku'alofa Police establishment who had been watching their unconstitutional activities by telescope for some hours. The lawbreakers were unfortunately within the three-mile limit, or a neat problem might have been posed. Upon being acquainted with the nature of his misdemeanour, one of the visitors was heard to remark with some acidity:

"Jees. These guys gotta constitooshun too. Then why the heck don't it say what I can do, instead of what I can't?"

The legislators of 1921 had not yet exhausted the talents of their draftsman. The churches of Nuku'alofa are scattered throughout the town, but one or two rival denominations had been too close for physical and spiritual comfort. As a consequence, the law went on to provide:

> Should the churches of two religious denominations be less than three hundred yards distant from one another the Minister of Police or mayor shall fix the time for holding their respective services so as to prevent churches so situated from holding their services at the same time. The following shall be the hours for holding services: From nine until ten o'clock a.m. and from three until four o'clock p.m. for one denomination and from ten until eleven o'clock a.m. and from four until five o'clock p.m.

for the other denomination and whoever shall infringe this regulation by holding or attending any service which is not in accordance with the provisions of this section shall on conviction be liable to a fine not exceeding four shillings or be imprisoned with or without hard labour for three days in default of payment.

Provided that nothing in this section shall be held to apply to midnight New Year services or services on fast days.

With intervals for food and sleep, it was thus possible to indulge in what virtually amounted to a continuous performance.

Zealous sectarian proselytising by the missions resulted in domestic fragmentation as Wesleyan minister, Anglican vicar, Roman Catholic priest, Seventh Day Adventist pastor and Mormon elder vied to retain or expand their flocks. We knew a family where the father was a Wesleyan, his wife was a Catholic and their four children all happily attended different mission churches and schools. The Tongan seemed to take this religious roundabout in his stride, revealing a spiritual adaptability impossible in a European family. A member of one church would transfer his affections without mishap if he lived in a spiritually mixed community. If, however, he lived in a predominantly Wesleyan or Catholic village where feelings on these matters could produce acute social stresses, it was not so easy. And the local *faifekau* or preacher was always on the spot to apply the screw.

The implications for others of an individual change of allegiance depended directly on the rank and influence of the person concerned. The church history of Tonga is marked by rifts and splinter groups, the effect of which is still felt. Political opposition to the Government has at times been identified with sectarian opposition to the established Free Wesleyan Church. Thankfully, it has not always been heavy with intrigue or fraught with dissension. An example with something of the humorous was that of Kasete, a man of minor influence in Nuku'alofa. He had for years been a staunch supporter of the Wesleyan Church. One day without overt warning, he upped and became a Seventh Day Adventist. There followed lamentation or gratified rejoicing according to one's point of view. It was for Kasete a decision of no mean consequence, involving as it did the renunciation, among other less important joys of life, of indulgence in roast pork and tea. The reformation necessary to effect this religious metamorphosis was accordingly profound.

Kasete "went over" and his friends settled down to see how long it would last. For a time, he stuck it without visible effect, apart from the loss of some of his waistline. Then one Sunday morning when he had been given up as a permanent loss, one of his former Wesleyan friends called at his house. To his surprise, Kasete was absorbed in trying to light a Primus stove. He had a wild gleam in his eye.

"You're not cooking on Sunday, Kasete?" was the horrified question.

"I am indeed," rejoined Kasete. "And furthermore, I'm making myself a cup of tea before I go to church. And it's not the church you think either. I've been dying for some tea for months. I'm going to drink this, I'm going to the Wesleyan Church again in ten minutes and when I come back, I'm going to eat a whole roast pig myself."

So, I believe, he did amid rejoicing and lamentation, this time in reverse order.

The Seventh Day Adventists celebrate the Friendly Island Sabbath on the first and not the seventh day of the week. The Adventist missionaries came to Tonga a little late in the game and were faced with the dispiriting entrenchment of the Constitution. If work and play were lawfully forbidden on Sunday, how could the new mission hope to attract a flock, if its own spiritual sanctions were to operate from sunset on Friday to sunset on Saturday? Furthermore, Saturday is the day on which the Tongan catches up on the planting and weeding he should have done during the week. A prohibition of Saturday work would result in unweeded villages and unplanted food crops, scarcely a productive line of appeal for a new church.

So the mission searched around for a solution; and it ultimately found one which was both practical and conscience-saving. The 180th meridian of longitude passes through the island of Taveuni in Fiji, about 400 miles west of Tonga. Tongan time, like that of

Samoa, should be about eleven hours after Greenwich; instead of which a decision was made to bend the meridian sufficiently far east to ensnare the Friendly Islands in the eastern time hemisphere. So today Tongan time is thirteen hours ahead of Greenwich. Far from being the country the furthest west from Greenwich, Tonga is, chronometrically speaking, the furthest east, plus one hour. This enabled the Adventists to assert without loss of face that time in Tonga should really be twenty-four hours or so after it was, no matter what the law said. Sunset on Saturday was actually sunset on Friday. So all was well and still is.

The problems of deciding what was Sunday and what was not Sunday were not, however, confined to the Church. The Minister of Police was finding that his prosecution of early Sunday morning revellers was meeting with scant success in the magistrates' courts. There were no convictions and he was becoming discouraged. More than a little incensed at the discharge of an accused for a palpable case of "conveying by waggon" one Sunday morning, he enquired the reason from the bench. He was informed that Sunday morning was, in law, not Sunday morning but Saturday night. Magisterially speaking, Sunday was from daylight on Sunday until daylight on Monday. Considerably shaken, the Minister sought the aid of the legal draftsman, and, shortly afterwards, with the approval of the Legislative Assembly and the assent of the Queen, there appeared an amendment to the Order in Public Places Act making it clear in black and white that, for the purposes of the Act, Sunday was henceforth from midnight on Saturday till midnight on Sunday.

All things Tongan being equal, that now seems to be that. But one thing is certain: if Sunday newspapers ever make their appearance in Tonga, they are unlikely to come out on the Sabbath.

14 The Cinema—Tongan Style

NUKU'ALOFA had three cinemas in our time. The first had half a roof and was really a garage—at least, it housed cars by day and showed films by night. At the entrance were a few pallid coloured lights and a *tapa* curtain through which you penetrated for the price of two or three shillings. Inside, a raucous "Tiger Rag" and a carpet of empty peanut shells. Most of the audience sat on wooden forms placed each evening on the concrete floor after the cars had been removed. If, however, you had paid three and not two shillings, you were led through an enclave lined with rows of corned beef tins to a wooden platform raised a few inches above the two bobs. There you had a cane chair instead of the form.

The second cinema was more pretentious. It was a two-storeyed wooden building with roof complete. A white flag with the letters "I. H. S." embossed in black, flapped languidly above it by day. I was told that I.H.S. meant "In His Service", but it was never made quite clear who "he" was and why and how he was being served. Inside, the plebeians were again seated on forms in the pit, while the patricians upstairs had moderately comfortable tip-up leather seats. The main disadvantage of these was that they were somewhat narrow for the bulky Tongan ticket-holder who could at least spread himself on a wooden bench. Two identical narrow wooden staircases led upstairs from inside the entrance. Since neither divulged its destination, you could find yourself in the projection room instead of the auditorium.

On my first visit to cinema number two, I arrived halfway through what appeared to be a 1934 Graham McNamee *Sportlight*. It was neither visible nor audible. There were less than twenty people present, a circumstance which became comprehensible when the misadventures of Mr. Bud Abbott and Mr. Lou Costello in Morocco were halted by projection blackouts four times in the first fifteen minutes. On each occasion the audience was blinded by a cluster of fierce electric lights and deafened by "Doggie in the Window" and "Tell me a Story" alternately, while the projectionist struggled with his obstinate machine. During these enforced intervals, the space on either side of the screen—there was no stage—was seen to contain a tangle of ancient iron beds and mattresses. These were, I supposed, for weary clients determined to stick things out come what may. After the fourth interruption, I felt my own evening was complete and found my way down the wooden stairs again.

I paid a second visit some months later, attracted by the proclamation outside the entrance that the Boulting Brothers' production of *Seven Days to Noon* was to be shown that evening at seven o'clock. Having ascertained that this was to be the first of two films, Margaret and I arrived a few minutes before the appointed hour. We bought our tickets, made our way up the correct staircase and found ourselves the sole occupants of the building. For ten minutes nothing happened. Then the loudspeakers went into battle at a volume sufficient to endanger the most robust eardrum.

The result was not, as we expected, to send every cinema addict in Nuku'alofa belting off to the lagoon to escape the bedlam. First, three small boys came in below. They made for the front benches, a few feet from the screen and its surrounding flotsam and jetsam. There they sat still and apparently unmoved by the racket, until the appearance of a slightly older plutocrat caused three pairs of deep brown eyes to turn enviously towards his ostentatious ice cream. Then at about seven-twenty, a male figure entered wearing hat and sun glasses—a precaution, we supposed, against the glare. The new arrival also walked to the front, placed his hat on one of the mattresses and returned to sit in solitary state some rows back. A few others joined us upstairs. A young girl appeared and asked for our tickets. She, it transpired, had come late.

There was still no sign of activity in the projection box behind us; and I began to have serious fears for the Brothers Boulting. Was it perhaps to be next Saturday, or worse, was it last? Some of the strength of the Tongan lies in his apparently inexhaustible patience in waiting for expected proceedings to begin; and those who enter his world from a less tolerant way of life have to adjust themselves accordingly—or get ulcers. So we too waited.

By seven-forty, the auditorium was a third full and there were about thirty little boys in the front seats. Above the third performance of "Lady of Spain" on massed banjos came a teutonic injunction to those outside to proceed within since it was desired to begin. An imposing official appeared before the boys and with much accompanying gesticulation exhorted them to gentlemanly behaviour on pain of expulsion. We rose for the playing of the Tongan National Anthem. The lights flickered and we were away. It was seven-fifty and, within seconds, the place was miraculously full. Happily, there were only two breaks in the film; but when London had, in the nick of time, been nobly saved from ignoble destruction, it did seem that noon had been coming for seven days.

The romantic aura of cinema number three went little further than its name—"The Waterfront Open-Air Theatre". It was a rectangular box of corrugated iron, but a short distance from the Nuku'alofa wharf. The ticket office was a square hole in the wall of iron sheeting. The interior consisted of a sand and sawdust floor, the inevitable two-shilling wooden forms (without backs) and three-shilling iron benches (with backs) for the opulent or the discriminating. Canvas sheeting replaced the stars above three-shilling heads. There was an iron cell at the back for VIPs. Movement from this involved the temporary effacement of the screen; and retreat in the darkness was a navigational problem.

Before the Royal Visit in December 1953, it looked as if the iron shell of number three might well collapse with age and disrepair. Although the building was not on the royal route, the time seemed appropriate to suggest improvement.

"Oh, yes," responded the owner with unexpected enthusiasm, "I'm very ashamed of it, as it is, and I'm going to rebuild completely."

"Fine," I said, "what with?"

"New irons, of course," he replied.

There was no concrete zone in an un-townplanned Nuku'alofa.

Programme advertising was generally done by means of a ragged poster or a chalked notice board outside the cinema.

Occasionally, however, the wheels of the publicity machine would grind and this, from the proprietor of the Waterfront Open-Air Theatre was, on cyclostyled sheets, the English language result:

FRIDAY NIGHT 27TH

"SOULS AT SEA"

STARRING

CARRY COOPER CARRY COOPER

One cannot forget the outstanding performances of this actor. This time he again acts the part of the hero. In this role, the fast moving action in this historical drama, reminds one of the other programmes of Carry Cooper; such as in the Plainsmen, Lives of a Bangle Lancers and the Unconquered.

Since this theatre, the Open-Air Theatre, had not screened any classical programmes for quite a while, we will screen this programme "THE SOULS AT SEA" for one week, starting from the 27th instant to the 3rd December inclusive.

We regret that we do not have any posters to accompany the advertisements of this very entertaining show; but with the name of this actor, I am sure that you will not have doubts in your mind the quality of the programmes.

On another occasion, the cyclostyled appeal read like this:

NOTICE—NOTICE—NOTICE—NOTICE

THE WATERFRONT—OPEN-AIR
THEATRE

The great film "SAMSON AND DELILAH" has at last arrived in Tonga. It is one of the greatest biblical stories which man has ever succeeded in producing as a movie and talkie. It is in technicolour and is hailed throughout the world as one of the greatest achievements of our epoch. See that you do not miss it and feel sorry that you do not see this great film. If you miss this opportunity of seeing "SAMSON AND DELILAH" you will not only lament it but will brood over it for the rest of your life. Although its cost of hire was and still is so terrificly high we begged for its hire since 1951 and it is here now for your entertainment and enjoyment.

The story depicted in this great film is of something which took place centuries and centuries before Christ. They were actually happenings one thousand years before Christ. The story concerned is found in the Book of Judges in the Old Testament in chapter 13 to 16. Read these chapters to refresh your memory of the Great Truth that the Bible presents for your own betterment and information so that you can enjoy this masterpiece film to the full.

The time which this great film can be screened in Tonga is so limited that this Theatre's management has decided to screen it nightly for three weeks in order to give every christian beings on our land the golden opportunity of seeing it. The three weeks showings are divided up as follows:

The opening night will be on the night of the 8th September, 1953, at 8 p.m.

Tickets will be sold as from the night of the 4th September, 1953, for any night of the first week. All tickets will be sold at the price of 2/-. Tickets for sale for one night will be limited to a certain number.

Limitation of sale of tickets for each night is in case any one buys a ticket and finds no seat. Ushers will be engaged to see that you are comfortably seated. While this great film is here we shall screen it every night except Sunday nights and any night it will rain.

It will be appreciated if the people of Kolofo'ou including Fasi and Pahu, Kolomotu'a and Ma'ufanga will endeavour to see the show on any of these nights, 8th to 12th of September, 1953 (First week). The Hahake, Hihifo and the Vahe Loto people may come on the night of the 14th to 19th of September, 1953. (second week). Should any of the country folks or of Nuku'alofa wishes to see the show in any other nights than those mentioned above can do so but only by obtaining a ticket for the particular night for which his ticket shows.

We will not allow any tickets that you may buy for a certain night on any other night but for that particular night dated on the ticket.

If it rains on any night from 6 p.m. to 8 p.m. we shall not screen "SAMSON AND DELILAH" but we will screen another instead.

The film of SAMSON AND DELILAH shall be interpreted as from the night of the 14th onwards for the benefit of the Tongan people. Those of you who understands English and are worried by the interference of the interpretation may come to see the show on the nights of the 8th to 12th September, 1953, when the showing will not be interpreted.

Drivers and Lorry owners are hereby advised to obtain the tickets for the people whom you shall bring lest the people come on a night on which they should not have come. Please see the ticket seller about the number of people your lorry will bring and to ascertain the night on which you are to come on lest some unexpected things happen.

Respectfully yours,
T. M. Niu,
Your obedient servant.

Regrettably, some unexpected things did happen. In spite of all his efforts, the theatre of this energetic impresario—whose surname means 'coconut'—has gone out of business and is now no more.

15 North to Vava'u

THE people of Vava'u have been called the Irish of Tonga. They are markedly different from their brothers of Tongatapu and Ha'apai—ebullient, extrovert, and skilled organisers of important customary occasions. The term *faka Vava'u* —in the manner of the people of Vava'u—is proverbial for what is proud or even boastful in the eyes of other Tongans. The northerners have an early history of turbulent rivalry. As they live some two hundred miles north of Tongatapu, they have had much independence from southern chiefly control. At various times in the past, their leaders were astute enough to share with Napoleon the view that when things get a bit hot at home, the thing to do is to divert the attention of the people to piracy and plunder abroad. Now that this is no longer encouraged, the Vava'uan is preoccupied almost exclusively with the local scene; and an impressive one it is. The principal town is Nei'afu, notable for the past glories of raiding expeditions and Lever Brothers. The harbour is the most captivating in the South Seas.

Tungi spoke one day in the office about the bestowal by Captain Cook of the name of "Friendly Island" upon Lifuka in Ha'apai. It was there that Cook and his crew were received with an outward show of hospitality in 1774. Finau 'Ulukalala, high chief of Vava'u, unsuccessful plotter of Cook's murder and notorious ancester of Tonga's Minister of Police in our time, perpetrated what Tungi called "probably the biggest lie in Polynesian history".

"During the festivities of welcome extended at Lifuka to the company of the *Endeavour*," the Prince said, "Cook asked his host whether there were any Tongan islands to the north.

'Ulukalala hesitated. 'Yes, to the north lies Vava'u; but I should not advise you to go. There is no safe anchorage for ships and landing is difficult.' Assuming the reply to be correct, Cook gave up all thought of sailing north, not knowing that he had been hoodwinked into by-passing the safest harbour in the South Pacific.

"'Ulukalala deliberately misled Cook," Tungi explained, "to prevent the discovery of Vava'u; for he saw in the white man a threat to his own influence in Vava'u and Ha'apai."

And the shoulders of the Crown Prince shook as he laughed hugely at Finau's cunning.

The channel through which ships feel their way follows a tortuous course past coral heads and interlocked volcanic islands rising sheer from both sides of deep water. Navigation to the tiny wharf is a puzzle to the visitor as the all too proximate hills slide by a matter of yards from the ship. From the dock, there seems to be no way out of the land-locked harbour which has all the appearance of a crystal mountain lake. The people of Vava'u are justly proud of this natural splendour and on sunny days the eye is enriched by the peerless blue of their Pacific Capri.

The town perches crazily on the side of the hill, a perpetual apology for being there at all. There are a few stores and trading posts, the usual hotch-potch of rusting iron roofs which, when first encountered, so disturb one aspect of the South Seas myth. The Governor's flag flies from above the heart of local law and order; and there on the wharf is the populace of the town and half the countryside held back by a nonchalant policeman. Nei'afu has the trappings of lively activity during the seven hours each month when the *Tofua* is in port. Boxes of bananas and pineapples are rushed on board with the bursts of frantic energy which is so characteristic of the Tongan. Landrovers, trucks and two saloon cars—there were no taxis—dash about in all directions. The schools appear to declare an unofficial public holiday. Within half an hour of the ship's departure in the early afternoon Vava'u returns to the slumber of its sedate introspection until the next monthly awakening.

I became aware at Nei'afu that the Tonga Department of Telephones and Telegraphs pursues its man with the determined zeal of the Canadian Mountie. The Chief Medical Officer and I were staying in the Government Rest House. On the third morning, I was awakened by a hand groping through the mosquito net and shaking my reluctant shoulder. It was still dark.

"*Makoni!*" hissed a voice, this being Tongan for "Marconi" and meaning "telegram", for reasons which will be obvious.

"*Makoni?*" I responded sleepily and told the messenger to put it on the table beside my bed. He retreated with alacrity into the gloom.

I opened both eyes and telegram and read "Leaving Ha'apai 3 pm today, arriving Vava'u 6 am tomorrow. Master Hifofua." The ketch was to take me back to Nuku'alofa. Knowing something of its temperamental habits, I had asked the captain to confirm his arrival time at Vava'u, so that I could adjust my programme in the event of delay.

I wondered why this apparently innocent telegram should be brought to me at such an hour. Then I looked at the technical jargon above the message where the recipient is told, if he can work it out, the whys and wherefors of transmission.

> Time of despatch—Ha'apai 0835 hours
> Time of receipt—Vava'u 0840 hours
> Date: the previous day

I read the text again and looked out the window at the harbour now overlaid with the evanescent light that precedes the sunrise. The *Hifofua* was tying up to the wharf. My watch showed a quarter to six. Telegram received at twenty to nine the previous day.

I saw the local wireless station superintendent only once before my departure. He averted his eyes and affected absorption in a coconut palm across the road.

I thought I had seen all that the cinema in Tonga had to offer until I went to Vava'u. On my first evening there, the Chief Medical Officer and I were sitting down to dinner when the stillness of the night was broken by the sound of a handbell being rung in the road outside. Was this, we wondered, the counterpart of the postman's whistle in Nuku'alofa which isn't the postman at all, but the method by which the fishermen of the town let you know that they have a catch for sale?

Half an hour later we heard the bell again and asked what it meant. It was, we learned, the means by which the local cinema owner announced that he was open for business that evening. So we decided to investigate.

The main street of Nei'afu follows the line of the hill and falls away sharply to the harbour. Along the seaward side was a long wooden building the front face of which was flush with the pavement. There was a large crowd outside but, as yet, no one within. On the roof was a wooden platform. On top of this a searchlight revolved. Below the light were three loudspeakers which suddenly burst into a military march followed by a flood of Tongan rhetoric which must have been audible in Samoa. Its object was to persuade the reluctant throng outside that this was their last chance of getting in before the performance started. The waiting crowd knew better and four more exhortations were needed before there was movement towards the door.

To enter, we found, was a precarious undertaking. Inside the door there was a drop of twenty feet. An eighteen-inch-wide staircase led into the pit below. Halfway down there was a ledge on which were two wooden chairs. A recumbent body lay beside them. To the right of the staircase were some seats and the projection box. After digesting all this, we watched from above the procession into the pit. The body stayed immobile. Then from among the gathering audience a string band started up, its players lounging on the wooden forms, strumming guitars.

Soon we were away with the news. It was neither visible nor audible. When we had compared notes, we concluded that North Korea had invaded South Korea and complications seemed likely to ensue. With the arrival of the main film, the body showed signs of life, arose to seat itself and began to interpret the soundtrack into Tongan by the simple expedient of shouting down what was being said from the screen.

On the way home, I barked my shin on the cinema generator which was planted astride the footpath a few yards from the entrance, like the Russian jeeps that used to be parked on the pavements of Vienna. An intriguing evening, the more so for a complimentary ice cream and Coca-Cola, served by the manager, in the middle of the road outside.

I first went to Vava'u in October 1954. The visit coincided with that of the elegant and personable Princess Mata'aho, whose father was the Governor, so I found it in unusually festive mood. There were ceremonial presentations of food, *kava* parties, feasts and concerts. The tributes came from various sections of the people, all anxious to demonstrate their pleasure at the arrival of the wife of the future King of Tonga. Groups of Tongans arrived from first light until well after midnight, bringing their gifts and understandably expecting in return the personal presence of the recipients as the gifts were offered to them in the customary way.

Gifts of all kinds are the foundation of much Tongan custom and tradition. Few there are who go to Tonga and do not find themselves both gratified and disconcerted by the generosity of their hosts. There are customary rules about important gifts. In the old days a gift received by a Tongan was always offered to the ruler of the land. An early example is the famous tortoise reputedly left behind by Captain Cook. Soon finding its way into the possession of the Sovereign, it so remained in the chiefly dignity of the Palace grounds at Nuku'alofa until its lamented demise in May, 1966.

Although this custom has inevitably lapsed somewhat today, its spirit still remains. At all customary ceremonies at which a member of the Royal Family or a noble is present, the biggest and the best of the food or gifts are put aside to be sent to the sovereign. Even the immediate members of the ruling house observe the custom. At the annual nobles' feast at Pelehake in 1954 prepared by the people of which Queen Salote's second son, Prince Tu'ipelehake, is the chief, an enormous whole roasted pig, chosen many months before, was lifted by twelve hard-pressed men into a truck. It was being sent to the Palace for presentation to the Queen.

It is not only on formal occasions that this is done. I went on a weekend fishing expedition in the open sea sixty miles or so north of Tongatapu. The results, with one exception, were disappointing. The exception was a sizeable tuna. Shortly before our return, the catch was divided up proportionately in accordance with rank among the members of the expedition. The tuna was washed clean of blood and dirt, wrapped in coconut leaves specially brought for the purpose and taken to the Palace for presentation to the Queen—the Tongan equivalent of the royal sturgeon in England.

The custom goes beyond the limits of Tongatapu, although the restrictions applied to Vava'u by the Government in order to prevent the spread of the voracious coconut palm-eating rhinoceros beetle now prevent the despatch of cooked food. "Live food" is, however, like human beings, presumed to be rhinoceros-beetle-free. From a colossal feast I attended in Vava'u when a cricket team from Tongatapu travelled north to play local opponents of long standing, the largest and fattest pig was left alive. I do not know whether pigs are subject to seasickness, but this one had to undergo a twenty-eight-hour voyage in not altogether Pacific seas before it reached its destination. It was sent to the Queen by the ocean-going cricketers. Whether or not a practice such as this can extend beyond the limits of Tonga is open to doubt. There are, I suppose, practical difficulties in the way of the presentation by a returning MCC team of a live kangaroo for consumption in the vicinity of the Long Room at Lords.

Another Vava'u cricketing practice is perhaps even less exportable. It has been known after a match of local importance for the defeated Vava'u Lancastrians to sit down in the middle of the pitch and proclaim their misery by weeping copiously for some minutes after their last batsman has been dismissed by a malignant Tongan Yorkshire. A tragedy such as this, especially when on home soil, will even infect the gaiety of the evening's post-mortem round the *kava* bowl.

An official certificate adheres to the back of the cricket bat I took with me on this expedition to Vava'u. Faint but still legible are these typewritten words:

> Certificate of Fumigation
>
> This is to certify that this package has been inspected on the 4th December, 1954, and is entirely free from eggs, larvae and adult Rhinoceros Beetles.

Regretfully, I cannot pretend that the bat has, in its history, been entirely free from eggs other than those of the predatory beetle.

Sunset at Haʻapai

The last portrait of Queen Salote, taken in July 1965, some six months before her death

16 Death of a Chief

THE son of King George Tupou II and half-brother of Queen Salote, Vilai Tupou was the most ebullient figure on the Tongan scene during our first eighteen months. He was devastatingly handsome in a true Polynesian way, tall, and unusually slim for a Tongan. At fifty-five and the father of four daughters and three sons, he bubbled with an extrovert energy which belied the convention of social reserve of many of the Tongan nobility. As the Queen's ADC, his charm and tact at Royal audiences were a comfort to the uninitiated. On these occasions, Vilai wore the uniform of Commandant of the Royal Guards and three pips glittered on the shoulders of his spotless white jacket.

No feast was complete without him and his smile was never sunnier or his laugh more infectious than when he was seated before an array of sucking pig, lobster, fish and yam.

For twenty years he accompanied Queen Salote when she drove in state from the Palace to open or close the annual sessions of the Legislative Assembly. His splendid physique and proud but never arrogant bearing matched that of the Queen herself as they walked from the entrance of the Assembly building to the dais from which the Speech from the Throne was delivered. The Speech was neatly typed on notepaper bearing the Royal Arms of Tonga. The sheets were attached to heavy board backing by flowing ribbons in the Tongan colours of red and white. After the Queen had mounted the dais, Vilai handed the Speech to her and stepped down behind the Throne.

He performed this service for his Queen for the last time at the opening of the Budget Session of the Legislative Assembly in 1954. No one realised then that a life of devotion to the monarchy of Tonga was about to be brought to an abrupt and tragic end.

Heavy rains had fallen early in December that year and water lay in miniature lakes on garden and lawn. On the night of the 15th December, the winds had come. They swirled round the Norfolk pines on the Palace foreshore and beat harshly through the opulent trees of the town. Next morning an opaque sun played make-believe of a tolerable day. At Kaitangi, the home of Vilai and his family, a servant girl saw that the week's laundry could wait no longer. At ten o'clock she began to hang out the clothes on the line across the yard, her feet covered by water which still lay six inches deep underfoot. As she came to the bottom of her clothes basket, she noticed a wire lying across the line and dangling loose below. She reached out to throw it away and her face froze in agony. She fell into the water, her eyes staring, her mouth agape and her fingers taut round the wire. Hearing her cry, a gardener rushed to her aid. As he grasped at her now saturated clothing he too collapsed, twitching, across her body.

Tragedy now added to tragedy as Vilai hastened from the house. Seeing the hanging wire, he seized a long piece of wood and tried to beat away the wire from the two bodies. But the wood, like everything else, was wet. As the electric charge ran through the wood to Vilai's fingers he slipped and fell. The deadly wire scorched through the thin shirt he was wearing and burned into the bare flesh of his chest. When yet a fourth would-be rescuer had collapsed and the screams of the household had brought the neighbours running, the power was at last cut off from the mains.

At eleven o'clock Vilai Tupou was pronounced dead. Two others had died with him, while the fourth was so badly paralysed that his life too was feared.

The news of the calamity spread like a forest fire and the gossipers in the streets were hushed into silence. A distraught wife and family consulted as to who was to bear the lamentable tidings to the Queen. With all such occurrences in Tonga, there is a customary answer. To someone falls the responsibility because of family kinship or rank. The task in this case fell to the Minister of Police, 'Ulukalala, whose father was cousin to King George II and who was in his own right closely related to Vilai. Their wives furthermore were sisters. When 'Ulukalala was called to Kaitangi, he knew at once that it was his duty to bear the melancholy tidings to the Queen. And so he went to the Palace, a solitary saddened figure, his own boisterous bonhomie, not far removed from that of Vilai, now stilled in sorrow.

Queen Salote was in her upstairs apartments with Ve'ehala when 'Ulukalala met Princess Mata'aho and asked if she would seek permission for him to see the Queen immediately. He was summoned to the Queen's presence and Ve'ehala left them together. Queen Salote, who had but a few months previously mourned the deaths of an uncle and one of her most trusted and loyal *matapule*, was plunged into deep family bereavement. Instructions were given to 'Ulukalala for Palace mourning and the arrangements for the funeral. As the old King's son, Vilai was to be brought to lie in state in the circular wooden building in the Palace grounds until but recently the office of the Private Secretary.

A major part of the customary preparations of chiefly funeral rites falls to the undertakers who form a distinct social class in Tongan society. Next in precedence following the noble landed aristocracy are the *matapule*, some of whose titles carry an endowment of land, but most of which do not. The *matapule* are traditionally the masters of ceremonies to the sovereign and each has his specific functions. In the days of the Tu'i Tonga, the spiritual Kings of ancient Tonga, the house of Tuimatalau was ceremonially responsible for arranging dances and festivities, while that of Tui-'amanave controlled the sports which included wrestling, racing and throwing the javelin. There were the navigators, the fishermen and the carpenters. One of the old Tu'i Tonga, with a more meticulous care for detail than his forebears, used to have a *matapule* for each particular type of fish he liked. If he desired to taste a schnapper or cod, he called for Kula to catch it for him; if a bonito, it was Tamanika. Ahale was responsible for waylaying sharks, Ika Foli for the smaller fish and Fofavaha was head of the net fishermen.

The undertakers, the *Ha'a Tufunga*, too, are a class of *matapule*. Their number is restricted to twenty and they are the masters of ceremonial death in Tonga. Lawaki is their head.

As the day wore on, they began to arrive at the Palace in response to the Queen's summons. They are not permitted to wash, change their clothes or touch food during the ten-day death ceremonies of a high chief. Each man comes with his family who feed and cleanse him during that period. In the evenings, his body is refreshed from the sweat of the day by a mixture of candlenuts and flowers which are chewed together into a sweet-smelling oil by his attendants. When he has removed his shirt and *ta'ovala*, his body is gently rubbed with this salubrious concoction and—as I can, from experience, testify—he is then a new man.

From throughout the main island and from across the sea, the people began their journeys to the capital bringing tributes of food, mats and *tapa* for the royal mourning. By nightfall, a vast concourse of people had gathered in or near the Palace grounds which are normally *tapu* to the ordinary Tongan. All wore the heavy coarse tattered mourning *ta'ovala* and many were clad in black.

Shortly before nine o'clock, Prince Tungi left in company with three undertakers and drove to Kaitangi. They returned with the body of Vilai to the Palace where another two undertakers waited to receive it with a great offering of fine mats which had been made ready there by command of the Queen. It was a sombre emotional scene dimly lit by an adolescent moon as it rose an hour later from the sea beyond the Palace and fitfully filtered through the trees which surround the Royal gardens. Hundreds of dark, mourning figures sat cross-legged in the gloom as they waited in silent vigil for the night to end.

It is the custom for the relatives and friends of a deceased commoner to keep watch beside the body on the first night of death. Throughout the hours of darkness the watchers sing the hymns and chants of bereavement. The emotional state of the singers produces a high-pitched edge to the singing and this, together with the ululation of the women, is distinguishable from all other evocations in Tonga.

This is not the practice when high chiefs die; and on the night of Vilai's death, all was silent in the Palace. The unnatural hush which settled over the whole of Nuku'alofa seemed to still even the dogs and the cries of the children. The relatives, family and friends gathered together in a shelter outside the circular wooden office where the body lay in state. One by one the Queen's chaplain and his ministers came to say prayers, but there was no singing.

Beside the bed on which Vilai's body lay covered with fine mats and *tapa*, four undertakers sat on guard. The others outside, separated from the rest of the watchers, sat drinking *kava* round the mixing bowl until it came their turn to relieve the attendants inside. Swathed in black, the two Royal sons of Queen Salote with Princess Melenaite took their places beside the body shortly after nine o'clock. The immediate circle then consisted of Prince Tungi, Prince Tu'ipelehake, Princess Melenaite, Vilai's wife Tupou Seini, his half-sister Adi Salote, Heuifanga Ahome'e, mother-in-law of Prince Tungi, 'Ulukalala and his wife Tuna, and Ve'ehala. Tungi and Tu'ipelehake left shortly after two a.m.; the others stayed till first light. The Queen remained alone with her grief in her apartments; and Princess Mata'aho, due to give birth to her third child within a few days, also did not join the mourners.

On the death of a father, Tongan custom imposes what may appear harsh restraints on his children. They are not permitted to sit beside or see the body of their father; in fact it is not until the time of the burial that they may enter the room where he lies to make their obeisances. They then creep silently inside and kiss the body. This *tapu*, which does not apply to their mothers, derives from the male position as the *'eiki* or head of the family. Even when he is alive, the children may not go near his bed or touch his clothes; and the higher the man's rank, the more rigidly the prohibition is applied and observed.

Prevented therefore from joining the mourners, the chiefly sons and daughters of Vilai, themselves all begetters of their own families, set about the menial duties which custom demanded of them. In order to affirm their humility in relation to their father, they temporarily assumed responsibility for the cooking and carrying of the quantities of food required to feed the undertakers and the relations of their mother. A root of green *kava* traditionally accompanies the food to the undertakers. Accordingly, Vilai's family was wedded to the kitchen and to labouring under the weight of heavy baskets of food. In the past, the domestic servant was the lowest rung in the ladder of Tongan social precedence. For ten days therefore, on such occasions, a chiefly birthright is renounced to a level beyond which there is no further customary debasement.

Meanwhile Lawaki and his undertakers had been busy. They had gone with Veʻehala to the chiefly burial ground to prepare the family vault to receive the body of Vilai. One of his daughters had died in 1938 and was buried outside the vault. Vilai had ordered that his daughter's remains were to be laid to final rest with his own when he should die. So the daughter's grave was opened and when the body had been exhumed it was covered with mats and *tapa*. Two undertakers stayed to guard the graveside until the burial service.

At four o'clock that afternoon I drove to the cemetery with its mounds of white sand set above the road along the foreshore beyond the Palace. It was a brilliant, silent day, disturbed only by the surf beyond the reef and a gentle trade wind which lapped lazily round the fretwork of leaves in the coconut palms fringing the shore. A mellowing sun, subsiding into the sea, glinted on a thousand brown heads sitting silently on the periphery of the cemetery. Above, two guardians of the grave sat as lonely sentinels of death.

The royal standard on the bonnet of a black limousine announced the arrival of Queen Salote. She was dressed in full mourning and the transient smile that acknowledged the bows of her subjects was stricken in sorrow. This was a Queen unknown to the London crowds, isolated in the inconsolable sorrow of human loss. Alone, she climbed the sands and was lost to the view of those below as she took her solitary place in the hollow of the ceremonial ground above. Thus, as always on the death of a close relative, did the Queen arrive first for the burial service.

A few minutes later the Police band began to lead the procession from the Palace grounds to the strains of the "Dead March" from *Saul*. A black arm-band set off each white uniform and black drapes covered the faces of the drums. Then the pall-bearers of the Royal Guards, their bodies bent beneath the weight of the great bier on which lay their dead Commandant surmounted with a breathtaking galaxy of the chiefly flowers of Tongatapu. Next the mourners—Tungi, Tuʻipelehake and their wives and the Ministers of the Crown. Then a space and the family of Vilai. Tupou Seini, his wife, her face sallowed with tears and coarsened with sudden grief, was barely supported by an attendant. The daughters, clad from shoulder to ankle in the great tattered funeral mats followed, their usually sleek raven hair pulled out and tangled. So transformed was one of the girls, who was my stenographer, that at first I failed to perceive her. Gone was the sophistication of an office world and the mind that coped daily with the routine of secretarial administration. She was a figure from another life, her head bowed in wracking sobs, her features distorted in Polynesian grief. Overnight the atavistic soul that lay dormant beneath the western exterior had been laid crudely bare. She was again of the Tonga of a hundred years ago, the plaything of the passions and emotions which can still surge over the fleeting veneer of the twentieth century. Yet, when she returned to her place behind the typewriter in the New Year, it was as if the tempest which had raged within mind, body and spirit, had never been. And we never spoke of it. Every day for eighteen months after Vilai's death, she came to the office clad always in black with the cumbersome shoulder to ankle-length mourning *ta'ovala*. How she coped with a dictaphone and produced impeccably typed letters for me under those conditions, I never knew.

Behind the relatives, the road was alive with people come to join those who were already at the cemetery. The obsequies began upon the hollow mound, witnessed by the Royal Family, the relatives and but a few others with specific functions to perform. Even the Ministers of the Crown remained below in respect for the great chiefs who lie buried there. The sanction extended even to 'Ulukalala because his father's grave is there. He might not approach it, for the sanctity owed to a father in his lifetime does not cease after death. After the funeral service had been read and the time came for the vault to be opened, a great length of tapa was unrolled and held up by helpers posted round a twenty yard square to screen the area from the eyes even of those nearby the vault. None but the undertakers may look upon the open grave of a chief and even those holding up the *tapa* did so with their backs turned to it.

When the vault was clear, they took Vilai in and his daughter and then closed the vault and buried him. The "Last Post" and "Reveille" were sounded. The band played the Tongan National Anthem, the Queen departed in her car and the grave was raised to a great mound of sand. Slowly and silently the people stole away and left the undertakers to decorate the grave with flowers and wreaths. Vilai Tupou had been laid to his last rest.

As the sun went down behind the Royal Chapel one evening, we stood at the seashore and watched a small cutter arrive on the beach. On the deck was a pile of giant clam shells, soon to be gutted of the white liver-like flesh that constitutes the living creature inside the shell. Beside the clams were flax baskets with white coral sand. I asked about the sand and learned of one of those intriguing aspects of Tongan custom found at unexpected times and places.

We had lived for two years between—as Atwell Lake put it—"a cemetery on the one side and a swamp on the other"—without appreciating that the sand placed on the top and round Tongan graves is not from the beaches of Tongatapu. The graves are sandy mounds built up two or three feet above the surface of the ground. The final sealing of the grave is its decoration with special white sand called *pata* which is laboriously dug and transported from outlying islands to the graveyards of Tongatapu. The period of normal mourning is ten days and during that time the near relatives of the deceased keep watch throughout day and night beside the burial place. The laying of the *pata* signifies the end of formal mourning. From that time onwards the unbroken vigil ceases and only periodic visits for grave tending are then paid.

Wherever custom plays its part in Tonga, there is one practice for the commoner and a variant of it for the chief. Eating, sitting, dancing and walking—virtually every function of daily life—has accepted sanctions on the commoner particularly when in the presence of his chiefs. Accordingly the graves of chiefs are bedecked with great scaffoldings of flowers, grass skirts and reeds which are renewed when the family and retainers pay their daily tributes at the graveside. When King George Tupou I died in 1893, hundreds of children of Tonga College, which the King had founded, and other schools lined the road from the Palace to the Royal tombs. Each child carried a flax basket containing the rarest of white coral sand; and after the body had been lowered into the vault the children came one by one to pour their baskets of sand on to the royal grave.

In addition to the white coral sand, chiefly graves are studded with black pebbles known as *kilikili* which are only obtainable from the tiny isolated volcanic island of Tofua about 100 miles north of Nuku'alofa. The magnitude of the funeral and the duration of mourning depends in each case on the importance of the chief who has died.

So for ten days each morning and evening, the undertakers accompanied Vilai's family to the burial site to renew the decorations and to place the final layer of fine white sand and black pebbles on top of the mound. After the final distribution of food, the mats and *tapa* which had been presented on the occasion of the funeral were divided up among the undertakers whose melancholy task was then done.

The Queen released her people from mourning on Christmas Eve 1954, but the shadow of Vilai's tragic death hung heavily on us all throughout those normally joyous days in Christian Tonga. It was to be so again—exactly eleven years later to the day—as the death of Queen Salote herself brought a deeper and all-pervading sense of national loss to every Tongan and to the world.

17 Private Secretary

IN the days before the typewriter came to Tonga, the clerks of the Government service were chosen according to the elegance of their handwriting. Whenever a new clerk was required, the Premier sent out to one of the colleges for samples of the handwriting of those who wished to be considered for appointment, and selected the one with the best copperplate. In the year 1879, the Premier was delighted to find in a youth called Fohe the possessor of a more cultured and dignified script than had yet graced the departments of his Government. So Fohe was found a post in the Premier's own office and from there his fame spread across the seas of the kingdom by means of the letters he drafted in his own hand for the Premier's signature.

For over ten years, Fohe remained secure in the light of authoritarian favour until one day, after he had also become office treasurer, the Auditor-General paid a surprise visit to the office. The auditor examined Fohe's books, counted the cash in the safe and was gratified (for he too prided himself on his hand-writing) to discover that there was a discrepancy of several pounds.

With a show of the greatest regret, the Auditor-General made his report to the Premier, who found himself reluctantly obliged to cast Fohe into servitude at the gaol.

While these melancholy events were taking their course, the old King, now aged ninety-two, had been pondering the desirability of the appointment of a Private Secretary. King George had not previously possessed a secretary all to himself. It had, however, been suggested by some of his advisers—each of whom had indicated how impossible it would be to find anyone more fitted for the post than himself—that it was in keeping with the dignity and status of the sovereign head of the State that he should be endowed with a personal scribe. The King finally made his decision to approve the proposal the day after Fohe had been banished in disgrace from the service of the Government. The Premier was commanded to the Palace and asked for his recommendation of a clerk suitable in every way to be chosen as Private Secretary to the King.

"Alas, Your Majesty," lamented the Premier, "I had until yesterday such a one—the possessor of the finest handwriting in all Your Majesty's realm and a man well-fitted to serve Your Majesty as he has served me for the last ten years."

King George was at this time very hard of hearing and the words "until yesterday" eluded his ear.

"Good. I appoint him, then," said the King, who having made up his mind to have a Private Secretary, now wanted to get the post filled as quickly as he could. "What is his name?"

"His name, Your Majesty, is Fohe," replied an embarrassed First Minister, "but he is in gaol and . . ." He paused and summoned all his resources of courage in order to continue.

"I do not know whether Your Majesty would think it altogether proper to appoint a *prisoner* to the post!"

The Premier's voice had sunk to a whisper and as he finished his sentence, his head dropped in shame for his temerity, as he sat cross-legged before his sovereign. A royal eyebrow lifted, but no reply was forthcoming.

Even at the age of ninety-two, King George Tupou I was not one to stand on ceremony. Without further ado, he summoned his driver, horse and buggy and ten minutes later was in full cry to the gaol. The Chief Warder, not knowing the cause of the visitation, sank on his knees as the King descended from the royal carriage.

"Pray bring the prisoner Fohe to me," commanded His Majesty.

The Chief Warder retreated into a nearby banana plantation and emerged clutching the fallen scribe.

"Are you Fohe?" asked the King, when the trembling wretch had been brought to him, "who is known throughout the length and breadth of my realm as the most elegant copyist of all my subjects?"

Since no man might disagree with the sovereign, Fohe murmured that something of the sort had, he believed, been suggested.

"Then," said King George to the Chief Warder, "fetch me the Book of Royal Pardons."

When the book had been brought, the King put his name opposite that of the prisoner "Fohe—embezzlement—three months."

Then he turned to Fohe and announced, "You, Fohe, I hereby appoint as the first Private Secretary to the King of Tonga and I call upon the Chief Warder of my prison on Tongatapu to bear witness to my decree."

And with that, King George climbed into his buggy, summoned his new assistant to follow behind, and returned to the Palace. There Fohe was permitted to remove his prison garments for attire more befitting the first Private Secretary to the King of Tonga.

More than half a century went slowly by. Queen Elizabeth and the Duke of Edinburgh paid their fleeting visit to Nuku'alofa and about a hundred local notables were presented to them on the public green beside the Palace and the seashore. The last to have the honour was a short frail old Tongan with parchment skin and still bright brown eyes. As he bent over the hand of the young Queen of the Commonwealth, Queen Salote was seen to whisper a word in the ear of her royal guest. The old man paused, caught for a brief exhilarating moment in the spell of royal interest as Queen Elisabeth smiled and spoke to him. Then with head bowed and eyes aglisten he went on his way; and the day reverted to the splendid excitement of less simple things.

Eighteen months later, the same old man sat in our house in Nuku'alofa and gazed at the ceiling as he cast his memory back to that glorious December in 1953 and to what, for him, lay before it.

"My presentation to Her Majesty Queen Elizabeth and His Royal Highness the Duke of Edinburgh," he said, "was my reward for long service to the Royal House of Tonga."

In 1955, Tongilava was eighty-two. He joined the Palace staff in 1898 as assistant to Fohe the first Private Secretary to King George Tupou II, who had succeeded his great-grandfather, George Tupou I, in 1893. Tongilava became Clerk to the Privy Council in 1903 and was appointed to succeed Fohe in 1905. He remained Private Secretary for forty-five years—firstly to King George II and later to Queen Salote. He retired in September 1950 at the age of seventy-seven, a matter of weeks after Tonga had, in traditionally lavish style, celebrated the fiftieth anniversary of the Treaty of Friendship with Great Britain. Over a period of sixty-one years only two men filled the post of Private Secretary to the Tongan Royal House. And the third, Maile Tonga, has so far held office for sixteen years.

The Royal Visit had passed into Tongan history when I went to Fiji for a few days in April 1954. The last accounts had been paid and the files had been put away, I thought, for the final time.

Two days before I left I was driving past the Palace when a collarless Private Secretary emerged on a bicycle and pedalled furiously towards me. Observing the ripple on the usually calm surface, I stopped and enquired what was up.

P.S. I am sorry to bother you, but Her Majesty has a letter from Queen Elizabeth.

K.R.B. I see. That's very nice.

P.S. Her Majesty wishes to reply to it immediately and desires me to ask if you would draft a reply for her to send off by the next mail.

K.R.B. What is the letter about?

P.S. It is a letter of thanks from Queen Elizabeth to Queen Salote for all that was done for the Royal Visit to Tonga in December last year.

K.R.B. When was it written?

P.S. On the *Gothic* after she left Tonga for New Zealand. The 22nd December, I think.

K.R.B. But this is now April.

P.S. Yes it is, and Her Majesty is therefore anxious that the reply should be sent immediately.

K.R.B. I understand. But I should like to know exactly what I am to draft a reply to. Have you the letter?

P.S. Ah . . . no.

K.R.B. Where is it then?

P.S. We cannot find it. I believe it may be lost.

K.R.B. For how long has it been lost?

P.S. Maybe since . . . January.

K.R.B. Then I suggest that you make a thorough search of the Palace office and the Palace itself.

P.S. I shall, immediately.

A dejected figure retreated into the Palace grounds, and I drove on. At noon next day we met again, oddly enough in the same place. The wheels of the bicycle were pointed triumphantly towards my office and the pedals were working overtime. The presence of a collar and tie was a good sign and a large white envelope in massive brown fingers even better.

P.S. We have found the letter and I have brought it to you as I promised.

K.R.B. Splendid. Where was it?

P.S. It was . . . under Prince Tungi's bed.

He smiled happily. His pleasure was in the recovery of the letter, not the circumstances of it.

When the draft had received the Queen's approval next morning, the faired copy was sent to the Palace for Her Majesty's signature. I boarded the flying boat soon after lunch and three hours later emerged again in Fiji. The Royal Letter, I supposed, nestled securely inside a mailbag on board.

Six days later I went back to Tonga, by Royal New Zealand Air Force Sunderland aircraft, travelling with Sir Ronald and Lady Garvey. He, as Governor of Fiji and Consul-General for the Western Pacific, was paying his first official visit to Queen Salote and her Kingdom since his assumption of office. For four days, we were absorbed in the affairs of his visit until the drafting of a farewell message from the Queen after his departure revived thoughts of another royal communication. I sought out the Private Secretary.

K.R.B. I suppose that the letter to Queen Elizabeth went away safely?

The Tongan strives to provide the desired answer to a question. Circumlocution in embarrassing circumstances and avoidance of being the source of unwelcome information is an essential skill for a royal private secretary. A sublime blamelessness lit up his face.

P.S. It has been dealt with.
K.R.B. Yes, but has it been sent?
P.S. It has been sent to Her Majesty.
K.R.B. And did Her Majesty sign it?
P.S. I am not sure.
K.R.B. But are you not Her Majesty's Private Secretary?
P.S. I am (proudly).
K.R.B. Then do you not know whether Her Majesty has signed the letter and whether it has been sent? (The innocence became radiant.)
P.S. I believe Her Majesty thought that the paper was not good enough for a letter to Her Majesty Queen Elizabeth.
K.R.B. The letter then has not yet left the Palace Office?
P.S. By the Queen's command, it has remained.
K.R.B. And new paper has been ordered?
P.S. The matter is receiving urgent attention.

A month later Queen Salote left for Ha'apai, some twelve hours' sailing north of Tongatapu. When elegant cream parchment arrived from New Zealand and had been embossed with the Royal Seal by the Government Printer, the letter was retyped and handed to the captain of the *Hifofua* for delivery to the Queen at Ha'apai. There it was signed and, after a ten-day journey in a rusty tin box round other ports of her maritime Kingdom, returned safely to Nuku'alofa and to me. Thence to the British Agent and Consul and, by means of the Colonial Office safehand bag, to Buckingham Palace in London.

This is the text of the letter:

The Palace,
Nuku'alofa
27th May, 1954.

I am deeply grateful to Your Majesty for your most kind letter written on board "Gothic" during the voyage to New Zealand. I am unable adequately to tell Your Majesty all that your visit and that of His Royal Highness meant to me, my family and the people of my Kingdom. For each one of us, it was indeed a dream come true and your graciousness in visiting these scattered islands will remain an indelible memory treasured by every Tongan.

I can but hope that I may one day again visit the heart of Your Majesty's great and abiding Commonwealth of Nations to whom Your Majesty's recent historic journey brought such profound joy and comfort.

Now that Your Majesty has returned safely to your home and family, I pray God that Your Majesty and His Royal Highness may long be spared to guide the people of your many dominions through peace and security.

SALOTE TUPOU

Sadly, Queen Salote never did realise her wish to return again to the London which had taken her to its heart and which she came to love so much in return.

18 The Legend of Sangone the Turtle and the Royal Mats

A LONG time ago, a man called Lekapai lived in Samoa. In his garden, he grew breadfruit, plantains, bananas, yam, taro and many other kinds of fruit and vegetables.

Then, as time went on, there was a great hurricane, and his plantation was almost ruined. After it was over, Lekapai set to work to replant his gardens. But alas, there was another hurricane the next year, and the next, so that three food crops were destroyed one after the other. Poor Lekapai became disheartened and after pondering what he should do, said to his relatives: "I shall go and try to find out where the wind lives, and ask why he seeks out and destroys my plantation."

So Lekapai launched his boat and sailed south towards Tonga where the wind comes from. After he had journeyed for several days he saw a big rock ahead of him. When he drew near to it, he could not find a landing place anywhere. So he sprang up, grasped the branch of a white-flowered pandanus tree, and managed to clamber ashore. He then saw a narrow pathway and followed it, down and down under the ground.

On and on he went, and presently, looking ahead, he saw a woman facing him. They say that she was a very beautiful woman. "Where do you come from?" she asked him, "and how did you find your way down here?"

"I have come," answered Lekapai, "to try to find out where the wind lives—the wind that keeps on destroying my garden."

"You have come to the right place," replied the woman. "The winds are my children. And if you wish to see them, come with me and I will call them."

"Thank you," said Lekapai, "for making my journey worth-while."

They went on a little further, and the woman called out: "Let the strong north wind blow this way!" And immediately it began to blow, becoming stronger and stronger.

"Let the whirlwind come!" the woman commanded. And the whirlwind began to sweep round and round.

"Let the gale come!" the woman called. And the coconut palms began swaying and snapping, and all around them trees of all kinds came crashing down.

"Let the hurricane come!" the woman called out. And once again the wind blew: and this time it was so strong that Lekapai could no longer stand against it, and the earth began to split, and great rocks began to fly. Lekapai was afraid and begged the woman to tell the winds to forbear and rest. "I don't want to see any more," he said. "I am nearly dead with fear. I do not mind about my gardens, I only wish to return home safely to Samoa."

So the woman spoke again. "Go away and rest," she said. At once the strong wind eased off, the sun shone again, and the breeze that now blew was warm and pleasant.

They then came back and went to the woman's home, and she told Lekapai that her name was Hina. "And mine is Lekapai," he said. Then Hina said: "Stay here for a while and when my mother goes, she will take you with her."

A few days passed, and Lekapai asked again to go back to his own country. "Then go and get some coconuts to take with you," said Hina. So he went and picked them.

When Lekapai came back, Hina was sitting there with a turtle beside her. "This is my mother, who is now a turtle," she said, "and will take you with her." If you should want a drink while you are out on the ocean, do not break your coconut on the turtle's head, but on its back. And when you reach Samoa," she added, "go and bring a piece of *tapa* cloth, and a bottle of oil, and a large coconut leaf, and give them to the turtle to bring back. Her name is Sangone, the sacred turtle. Do not betray her or evil will surely befall you and your family."

They then said goodbye, and Lekapai mounted on the turtle's back, and Sangone swam with him out to sea. Soon Lekapai became thirsty, and not believing the truth of Hina's story or caring to obey her, he took a coconut and broke it on the turtle's head. When they reached Samoa, he took the turtle ashore, killed it and cut it up, and divided it out among his relatives; and the shell of the turtle they buried secretly beside a candlenut tree where no one could find it. Then, noticing that a boy named Lafaipana had observed them, Lekapai called to him to come. When the boy came running across Lekapai put out his hand and laid it on Lafaipana's head, and said: "So that you may not reveal my secret, you will be Little Lafaipana: slow be your growth, and small your stature! And the day that Sangone the Turtle is found, you will die!"

So Lafaipana grew very slowly; and he soon forgot the threat about his death. For he was but a boy and death has no meaning for children.

Many, many years passed and then the Tu'i Tonga heard a rumour of what had happened to Sangone the Turtle in Samoa. He gave orders for his younger brother, Fasi'apule, to go to Samoa and find, if possible, Sangone's shell, and return it to Tonga. So Fasi'apule set out. When he reached Samoa, however, he could not find anyone who seemed old enough to remember where Sangone had been buried. So, after drinking *kava* with the Samoan people in accordance with the custom of the land, he gave them a riddle to solve. "Guess this one," he said. "O that I might drink a clap-it-and-it-smokes!"

So they all began asking one another what he meant. Then finally, Lafaipana, now a very old man, told them to go and bring some tiny pieces of dried *kava* root which sends up dust like smoke when they are clapped between the hands. So they brought some and gave them to Fasi'apule; and at once he began to wonder whether there was an old person still living who had solved the answer to the riddle and who might know the secret of Sangone's burial place.

The pieces of *kava* root were then pounded and mixed with water. They drank this, and Fasi'apule gave them another riddle. "Guess this one," he said. "A stalk fainting in the forest."

So the people ran to Lafaipana and asked him what it meant. "Go and find a bunch of plantains that has fallen and ripened lying on the ground out in the forest," he said.

So they searched and found one, and gave it to Fasi'apule. He was delighted, and gave them yet a third riddle to solve. "Guess this one! A leaf that tings. Guess that! A leaf that cries and makes a noise like a parrot."

They asked Lafaipana again, and he told them to bake a fowl and wrap it in young taro leaves, which make a faint tinging sound when they are stripped. This they prepared and brought to Fasi-'apule, and he gave them still another riddle. "Guess this one. Grunting and lying down."

They ran and asked Lafaipana, and he told them to bake a huge pig that was no longer able to stand, but just lay down grunting all the time. So they killed a great big pig and baked it, and took it along to Fasi'apule. Then Fasi'apule knew that there was an old and wise person who could answer the riddle of Sangone's hiding place.

So he asked the people who it was that had enabled them to solve his riddles. "It was Lafaipana," they confessed. So he ordered them to bring him. When Lafaipana sat before him, Fasi'apule asked him whether he knew where Sangone the Turtle was buried. "I know the place," he replied, "and I will lead you to it."

So off they went, and Lafaipana directed them to the candlenut tree, where he had gone so many years before. They dug down, and found that he was right. And it is said that when Sangone's shell was brought from the ground, it shone almost like a flame. As soon as it appeared Lafaipana cried out and fell dead. And they buried him with fine mats in the grave of Sangone.

Fasi'apule and his attendants then made preparations to return to Tonga. The Samoan chiefs, recognising the rightful ownership of the Tu'i Tonga, gave him two finely woven mats to accompany the shell of Sangone on its journey south to Nuku'alofa.

As soon as Fasi'apule arrived back in Tonga, he took the shell, as custom required, to give to his brother, the Tu'i Tonga. And the Samoan mat which he presented with it was called Hau 'o Momo (the honour shown to Momo). The other mat, however, Fasi'apule took to a cave and no man knew where it was hidden.

As time went on, Fasi'apule became old and died. Shortly

afterwards an elderly woman, on her way to the sea to get some salt water, saw the second Samoan mat spread out on top of a bush. So she folded it up and took it home with her and put it away.

Then one night, a *matapule* of the Tu'i Tonga dreamed that Fasi'apule came to him and told him that they should go and get the mat from the old woman: for it was a finely woven mat, the fellow of the one known as Hau 'o Momo, and its name was Laumata 'o Fainga'a (the eyelid of Fainga'a).

Messengers were sent to retrieve the mat from the old woman, and she explained to them how she had found it. After that the care of the two fine mats became the responsibility of the Tu'i Tonga and his people; and so these precious relics have been handed down, generation after generation, right up to the present day.

At the marriage of Queen Salote in 1918, her husband Uiliame Tungi wore ten fine mats wrapped round him, including those two historic mats brought long before from Samoa with the shell of Sangone the Turtle.

And at the joint wedding of the Queen's two sons on the 10th June, 1947, Crown Prince Tungi wore the mat called Laumata 'o Fainga'a, while his brother, Prince Tu'ipelehake, wore the one called Hau 'o Momo.

19 Round Trip

In May 1955, I went to Fiji on another sort of journey; to represent the Government of Tonga at a review of the terms of the agreement under which the South Pacific Health Service had been established in 1946. The member territories were New Zealand, in respect of its island territories, Fiji, and the Western Pacific High Commission administrations of the British Solomon Islands Protectorate, the New Hebrides and the Gilbert and Ellice Islands Colony. Tonga had accepted a subsequent British invitation to join in. The agreement provided for the recruitment of medical and nursing staff for the territories concerned; and for the co-ordination of medical and public health policy under the supervision of an Inspector-General who was also Director of Medical Services in Fiji.

Suva is about as far from Nuku'alofa as London from Edinburgh, but the *Tofua* indulges in a seven-day investigation of the ports of some of the northern Polynesian neighbours of Tonga to unload general cargo and to pick up bananas.

We sailed out between the reefs of Nuku'alofa harbour to a week of the most pacific Pacific I had experienced. The Hawkes Bay sheep farmers, escaping the minor rigours of a New Zealand winter, constituted a formidable part of the ship's passengers. They went ashore at each port wearing heavy trousers held up by thick braces. At the end of their voyage, the farmer and his wife returned to their homeland farm having learned for all time what went on "up in the islands". For my part, I found post-port conversation a good deal more trying than the gentle lullaby of the ship.

A night at sea and we were at Vava'u. The tourists went off in a gush of chatter to the Swallows Cave, a magnificent Capri-like grotto in Vava'u harbour.

"More swallows on the Tongan eightpenny stamp than in that cave," they said when they returned.

I got the impression that they thought that I was somehow to blame. Assurance that normally there were hundreds of swallows in the cave was little comfort. Tourist attractions are the same the world over. It is tedious to be told by some wise local, "Ah, but you should have been here last week! It was so much better then."

We emerged from the glorious harbour of Vava'u the same afternoon and sailed east to a tiny isolated dependency of New Zealand, Niue or Savage Island. The Niue Islander lives in the middle of a Pacific nowhere. Shortly after nine o'clock we dropped anchor off a rocky foreshore and, to judge by the swell, were still in mid-ocean.

The oval-shaped island is built, as the Resident Commissioner put it, "like a three-tiered wedding cake". There are no beaches and no wharf, no harbour and no reefs. The Pacific rollers crash with feckless abandon on this little Polynesian outpost, whose nearest neighbour westwards is Tonga and east—South America. The monthly call by the *Tofua* formed the only link with what lies beyond the timeless Pacific. No air service has so far been possible for the jagged island is heavily wooded. A passing aircraft is a hilarious rarity. On one occasion, a Tasman Empire Airways Solent flying boat was returning to Fiji from Tahiti. The pilot circled round the island at 2,000 feet, upon which the Resident Commissioner's house-girl fled indoors to emerge a few minutes later in a bright new dress and a revived hair-do. "She was," she stated emphatically, "in no fit state to be seen by the passengers on the aeroplane."

The *Tofua* stood off about two hundred yards from the landing. The shipping company made no bones about what happened next. "Passengers are warned"—surely not against exploitation, tubercular water or loose women, I wondered—"that they go ashore at their own risk. No responsibility can be accepted by the owners." The sheep farmers blanched a little and protested that they hadn't been told about this at the shipping office. Yet off we went in relays of small motor-boats which bobbed about below the gangway and showered us as they raced shorewards. We leapt from the crest of the swell to a terraced concrete causeway; and everyone said wasn't it exciting and one felt just like the ancient Polynesians riding the reefs, so to speak, didn't one.

It is not the passengers but the cargo which is the real problem at Niue. Cargo is unloaded by the ship's gear on to a platform lashed more or less securely across two narrow canoes. Since the platform rises, falls and slithers sideways at the whim of the turbulent sea, dropping and securing the cargo at the right moment requires skilful timing. After the crates are lashed together, the canoes are rowed to the causeway while the platform does things no marine insurer should ever know about. The canoes tie up against the causeway and the task of unloading begins as the open sea crashes the canoes against the fenders. At the edge of the causeway is a simple block and tackle which is lowered by a hand winch and attached to a crate. At the far end of a wire hawser, a tractor waits. When all is ready, the tractor steams off full pelt up a steep concrete ramp and so shuttle-hauls the cargo ashore. It is a masterpiece of improvisation; and in spite of the hazards involved, the Niueans manage to land between fifteen and twenty tons of cargo an hour. This happens only once a month, which may well be enough for the peace of mind of all concerned. There are trucks, motor-cars, tractors and bulldozers on Niue; and I still find it hard to believe that they were all safely landed in this way.

The Resident Commissioner is responsible to the New Zealand Minister for Island Territories for the administration of his flock of some 6,000 Niueans and a handful of New Zealanders. The island has an area of 64,000 acres criss-crossed by about 100 miles of road. Captain Cook discovered Niue in 1774 and British sovereignty was proclaimed over the island in 1900. In the following year, when the Treaty of Friendship between Britain and Tonga was ratified, Niue was annexed to New Zealand.

The Niuean is a far cry physically from his amply proportioned Tongan cousin. The people of the island are slim, short and wiry. Oddly enough they have no hereditary chiefs, a tradition common, so far as I know, to all other parts of Polynesia. Each family head has a status equal to that of any other. The people are as much New Zealand subjects as the residents of the Dominion and, unlike the Samoans, may travel freely to and from New Zealand. They are, for Polynesians, poor singers and their dancing is a hybrid conglomeration of the Cook Islands, Samoa and Tonga.

If they do not excel in the cultural arts, they are industrious and original workers. Niue fans and baskets are some of the finest and most elegant in the Pacific. The island has developed a minor export trade in these articles which are sold to tourists in Fiji at prices beyond the imagining of any Niuean.

Local houses are cheap and easy to build. The traditional method is using burned coral and local timber. A pile of coral is heated by a steady fire for about three weeks and then crushed into a kind of cement. This is mixed with water and pasted like plaster over a trellised framework. A finishing coat of coral whitewash is applied and a neat durable house has been built. No Niuean is faced with the problem of time-consuming thatch repairs which is a feature of Fijian and Samoan village life. Education is compulsory; and schools, which are free and secular, are built by this method.

Following the New Zealand practice, every school child receives a free glass of milk each day. All thirteen villages are visited by the Chief Medical Officer and the Child Welfare Sister once a week. If urgent medical attention is required, a red flag is placed beside the circuminsular road to attract attention. Communications are the essence of simplicity. There are none of the maritime hazards of Tonga, with its 150 scattered islands, or Fiji, which has about 300. A telephone line runs round the island. If the Resident Commissioner wishes to send a message to all villages, he makes a general call to thirteen village constables in whose homes the telephones are installed.

We had become accustomed in Tonga to a variety of refreshingly original Christian names. Successive garden boys were called Mustard, Sunshine, Primrose (not inappropriate) and Kaloti or carrot (most appropriate). We had a Sinamoni (Cinnamon); and I discovered a coalblack Solomon Islander one day rejoicing in his exile in the name of Eskimo.

The head gardener at the Nuku'alofa hospital was Pifalati, which is B flat. Maybe he had musical ancestors. So too I suppose had a taxi driver called Violin who could be summoned by calling the telephone operator, with whom he had an "arrangement".

In Niue, I heard of numbers of Tarpaulins, Kalasinis (kerosene) and even a Lumbago, inflicted, I suppose, by a suffering parent on his innocent offspring. Kilisimasi Tina (Christmas Dinner) was not uncommon; but I should award the prize to the Resident Commissioner's clerk who one day graduated to possession of a permit which enabled him to buy a modicum of liquor each month. Overjoyed at this recognition of his social status, he hied himself to the liquor store and bought six gaily labelled bottles. Even more enamoured of life three weeks later when his wife presented him with a daughter, he determined to perpetuate jointly the memory of both events. For the first time, he examined the labels on his now empty bottles and solemnly bestowed the name "Sparkling Cider" on the new arrival! I hope she has lived up to it.

From Niue, the *Tofua* headed north-west to the Samoas: American or Eastern Samoa first and then Western Samoa, at that time still administered by New Zealand. Separated by only sixty miles of open sea, the face of each was indelibly stamped with the way of life of the people of the administering Governments.

The broad peaks of Tutu'ila, the main island of American Samoa, rose hazily out of the ocean eighteen hours after we had left Niue. The menace of thick rain clouds hung in the air as the ship eased her way through the narrow entrance into the miniature circular harbour of Pago Pago. The harbour was once the crater of a great volcano whose seaward wall fell away centuries ago. Great green hills covered with dense tropical foliage slope steeply down to the water's edge. After the quiet isolation of Niue, Pago Pago was a pulsating, brash wayport of the Pacific. The township, which housed the American Navy for so long during and after the war, lies hot and thirsty at the base of a cluster of thickly wooded hills. Across the harbour the rain squalls race with sudden ferocity and the heat strikes up harsh and damp from the macadam sidewalks. The mother ship of a Japanese tuna fishing fleet lay beside us as the *Tofua* nosed into the wharf. A gaily-clad crowd waited behind a rope, held in check by Samoan cops clad in tight fitting American service khaki and carrying batons and pistols. "American Samoa" was proclaimed from motor-car plates, stores, the bank, street notices, Government departments and juke-box joints. An outsize limousine sailed by with a heavily starred two foot plate front and rear. "GOVERNOR", it said aggressively. On the sidewalk markets, silent Samoan women made no apparent effort to sell shoddy handicrafts. Enquiry into the prices soon dispelled the possibility that the dollar had escaped the attention of the ancients who sat smoking local cheroots and Lucky Strikes. In the stores, American accents rolled easily from Samoan lips. I passed an idle minute in gossip with a soft-spoken Fijian girl, perplexed and lonely in this strange new Polynesia. The braces went by a-glitter in the raw sunlight, clutching Arrow shirts and nylon stockings.

Within the whitewashed walls of the London Missionary Society church swelled the resonant voices of a Samoan choir, extending their welcome to a pallid pastor and his wife, installed on a dais at the head of the nave and but fifteen minutes before, struggling through the Pago Pago customs. In the rubble beside the entrance lay a heap of discarded bottles of Lucky Lager beer.

Over the way, a paint-starved wooden barn, swinging doors and a faded sign—"The Pago Bar". The choir finished its anthem of praise and the Hawaiian war chant drowned the motor horns. I pushed open the door. It was a square room, with three small windows, two long trestle tables and benches, a service bar, a few worn-out tarts and the total establishment of the ship's stewards. I placed a dollar bill in the wash on the bar counter and ordered a beer. A bottle spun towards me and some small coins. I asked for an opener and, after a pitying look from the other side of no man's land, got one. I had teeth, didn't I?

Hesitating again, I murmured that I should greatly appreciate a glass, if that were possible too.

"Glass? No glasses. We drink out of the bottle here!"

"Of course. I'm sorry. We drink out of the bottle, don't we. I should have known."

I sought a vacant corner and tried not to look too prim. From there the bar was happily concealed by the fudge from twenty newly opened packets of Camels. The band was blary, the sailors bawdy and the girls tough. Not for nothing had they coped for so long with the U.S. Navy. The *hulas* were raucous and rude. Bottle in one hand and the other round a sweating brown waist seemed the game.

A two-hundred-pound madam presided at the door and smacked countless bottoms in the process of whipping up music, dancing and more beer. Two street urchins crept in under the swinging doors and were propelled backwards into the street by an elephantine foot. A shortsighted New Zealand grandmother, attracted perhaps by the sounds of revelry within, tentatively crossed the threshold and adjusted her eyes to the gloom. Concluding that even at her age she lay in imminent danger of mortal sin, she turned and fled, dragging a querulous child behind her. The mountain at the door shook with uncontrollable laughter. Through a window, a Samoan barber could be seen putting the finishing touches to a client's hair. Neither betrayed the remotest interest in the inferno within.

The bottles sped across the counter, the shrieks grew in volume and hands crept lasciviously into forbidden places. The motions of the early stages of the sex act became commonplace. A half-clad steward hiccoughed down my neck and confided thickly "If you don't get o' here, you'll bloody well get raped y'know." There was probably something in what he said and I made to withdraw while there was yet time. A taste of local colour was one thing; to wallow in it was unnecessary.

I stumbled out, blinking, into the white sunshine. It was just four o'clock. The church bell clanged and a siren rose and fell. Shop assistants crowded into the streets. For them, another boat day was over. They must have been made of sterner stuff than I; one was enough for me. I went and sought solace in a shoe-shine.

We sailed at six, personally farewelled by the Chief of American Samoa's Police, resplendent in tropical khaki, gold braided hat, truncheon, revolver and holster and smoking an outsize Churchill cigar.

I now understood the look in the captain's eye as he had answered a question the day before:

"Do you ever stay after dusk in Pago Pago?"

"Never," he replied grimly—"if we did, I should never get the crew back on the ship."

20 The Government College

A FAINT but satisfying aura of glory distinguished the prisoner returning from the relaxing atmosphere of a Tongan gaol. No social stigma attached to him; in fact he was a bit of a popular hero, and his tales of life within what was known as the "government college" were relished by the less fortunate.

The main gaol of Huatolitoli was set comfortably in the country amid coconut palms, banana trees and well-kept lawns. There were no fences and no walls, no armed guards and no boulders to crack. Good conduct marks, with the consequence of premature release, were doubtful bounty. In the old days, prisoners went outside the prison to work each day and had to be back at the gaol by "closing time". If they were late, they were locked out. This was regarded as just punishment for late-comers, who thus missed their supper, their bed, and their breakfast.

The absence of prison walls was put to good use by one long-term prisoner some years ago. Over a period of months, a series of nocturnal burglaries occurred in Nuku'alofa. On each occasion, a card was left behind on which was written the solemn words—"The Red Hand Strikes Again". Nothing the police could do seemed to lead to the culprit. Every suspect invariably had a perfect alibi. Then one day in the gaol, a prisoner's clothes' locker collapsed—beneath the weight, it was discovered, of all the booty stolen in the burglaries. The "Red Hand" was a resourceful prisoner who had left the gaol each night, got his haul, and brought it back unnoticed to the gaol while it was still dark. After the locker collapsed, however, the Red Hand struck no more.

Daily prison duty in Tonga consisted of leisurely gardening on the prison plantations or the gay abandon of a truck journey into Nuku'alofa, where the chosen few were assigned to duty in the gardens of Queen Salote's Palace. In the penitentiaries of some less laudable lands, prisoners are distinguishable by their shaven heads. Tonga has an independent approach to such matters of protocol: so the guests of the Government are denied their hair-cut. You could tell how long they had been in gaol by the length of their hair. Apart from this, and their air of boisterous good health, they would not be recognised as wanton evildoers.

On admission to college, the new boy finds himself in a quandary. If he is sufficiently inactive, he will clock up good conduct marks; and will accordingly be ejected prematurely, to make his way again in the chill world beyond the non-existent prison gates. If, on the other hand, his behaviour does not measure up to the requisite degree of indolence, he may find he is not selected for Palace garden duty and may thus languish in the country without daily excursions into Nuku'alofa. The best thing is to ensure before you fail to pay your poll tax, and so pass the qualifying examination, that the Chief Warder can be claimed as some sort of remote relative; in which event, you may get the best of both worlds—Palace duty, no good conduct marks and a long college course.

When I arrived as a District Officer in Fiji in 1949, part of my duties consisted of being superintendent of the local gaol. This was also an unexacting "home-from-home" for its inhabitants. Straight, as I then was, from the sterner stuff of Palestine and the Middle East, my first visit to the gaol was something of a revelation. I was greeted with the midday sight of six Fijian prisoners lying fast asleep in the road-side grass, while the sergeant warder wielded an industrious cane knife. I am to this day not quite sure why.

As I opened the door of the charge-room in the tiny gaolhouse, two clucking hens fled through the window. The chief warder, who was a stately Sikh in beard and turban, satisfied his conscience by brushing away a few frayed feathers from the table. He then brought in his wife who, I saw, was engaged in some intricate needlework, which I admired. I should have known better. On my next visit, I was presented with a white pillow slip on which the warder's wife had embroidered in bold bright colours the words "Love Me Forever". I accepted this challenging gift with as much composure as I could muster. Later, I caused it to be hung out on my clothes line and watched the doubts arise in the minds of my neighbours as to whether my then bachelor state was all that it seemed to be.

Tonga is never consciously outdone by Fiji in matters of this sort. In the Palace grounds at Nuku'alofa there were three swings built for use by Queen Salote's grandchildren. At least, that is what they were supposed to be for. On one occasion when I passed by, the swings were going full bore, propelled by some hilarious prisoners. A few yards away, a plump and perspiring warder lay beneath a paw-paw tree, a handkerchief carefully laid over his eyes. As Princess Mata'aho once said—"The best way to punish these prisoners is to take them away from the Palace."

One of the more engaging privileges granted to Tongan prisoners occurs just before Christmas. One day I noticed a file of young men wearing khaki shorts and shirts, each stamped with a large number like the jerseys of football players, going into one of the stores in Nuku'alofa. It was not the football season. "Just prisoners," 'Uliti told me, surprised at my surprise. Were they perhaps in search of contributions for prison charities? Oh, no. The State was according them the courtesy of their customary annual shopping expedition to buy their Christmas presents.

The most eagerly awaited event of the college year is Old Boys' Reunion Day on which is held what is called the Annual Picnic. Our introduction to this occasion came by means of a printed invitation card from the Government Chief Jailer, the Warders and wives of the Huatolitoli Farm Committee. The picnic took the form of a gargantuan Tongan feast with a beaming Minister of Police as host, maître-d'hôtel and culinary adviser all in one. For weeks before, the gardens were deserted while the prisoners engaged in extra-curricular activities such as fishing, pig-hunting and lobster-trapping. Ex-inmates were specially welcome at the picnic. Old Boys the world over are notoriously critical; so that if there were 80 pigs, 200 fish and 50 lobster last year, there must be 90 pigs, 220 fish and 60 lobster this year.

In addition to the Old Boys, the Board of Governors was also present. A prominent member of this body was the Judge of the Tongan Supreme Court. The temporary holder of this post had but recently arrived in Tonga. He had sat for several weeks on a

People arriving in Nukuʻalofa for Queen Salote's funeral. All wear the tattered *taʻovala* of mourning

Part of the silent assembly awaiting the funeral procession

A Polynesian greeting: His Royal Highness Prince Tuʻipelehake greets his uncle Ratu Edward Cakobau, who has just arrived from Fiji to attend the funeral

difficult case of alleged murder. On the day before the Prison reunion, he had delivered judgment. The prisoner had raged, pleaded, threatened and wept, but had been sentenced to life imprisonment for manslaughter.

At the picnic, the Judge found himself in a place of honour among the rows of guests who sat cross-legged on mats before the mountains of food. The pork, lobster and fish were dismembered and placed before him by a young man wielding a sharply pointed knife. His mind on other things, it was not until he was halfway through the feast that the Judge began to reflect that there was something vaguely familiar in the appearance of his attendant. Tongan faces still seemed much the same and he asked whether they had met each other before.

"Yes," said the youth with a polite smile, "I am deeply honoured to serve you, Sir. You sentenced me yesterday to life imprisonment for manslaughter."

The Judge turned to the Minister of Police and asked whether the Minister was aware who the attendant was with the long pointed knife.

"Of course," replied the Minister with a satisfied smile. "I specially selected him to serve you since I knew you had already met."

The Judge stared in unbelief but could find no suitably judicial response. It was observed by those nearby that he suddenly lapsed into silent meditation and, for some reason, chose to cut up his own food for the remainder of the feast.

21 Those Were the Days

It is said with some truth that the Polynesian way of life is bound up in the three fundamental elements of human existence—birth, marriage and death. The contemporary observer might perhaps add a fourth—the auction sale. Occurring albeit spasmodically but, for the Friendly Islander, rather more frequently than the other three, the Tongan auction sale is Middle Eastern in the fervour, if not in the bargaining skill, of the participants. The Tongan lives domestically and financially for the day. At an auction sale, he lives for the moment—the supreme moment when he disgorges an outrageous sum for an unnecessary article and thus achieves that peerless but short-lived satisfaction at having beaten a persistent rival.

Bessie Leger, large, heavy, sleepy and masculine, was chief auctioneer in Nuku'alofa. He was equally well known for his unconventional domestic arrangements and his wickedness on one notable occasion in escorting an uninvited paramour to the Annual Ball of the Nuku'alofa Club. Bursting with righteous indignation, six censoriously-minded members posted a notice demanding a special general meeting to deal with the outrage; and to consider the desirability of Bessie's expulsion.

Came the evening, a goodly gathering at the club and an acting President in the chair. The assault was well under way about morality and the impropriety of the member named on the charge sheet when the door opened and in walked the accused himself. In the ensuing consternation, the prosecution case was brought to an embarrassed halt.

"Ha," said Bessie, "lot of people here tonight. Very solemn. Annual meeting? Thought we'd had it."

The silenced advocate looked to the chairman, now in obvious discomfort.

"Matter of fact, Mr. Leger, it's a special meeting on a rather important matter of principle," he ventured.

"Oh," boomed Bessie, "principle, eh! 'm all for principle. Always vote for principle, matter o' fact." And he sank heavily into a vacant armchair.

The chairman had recourse to the club constitution but found it silent on the requirement of sobriety on the part of all members present at a special general meeting. Bessie's eyes began to droop.

"Mr. Chairman," the prosecution resumed, "I do not think it proper for the meeting to discuss such a delicate matter as the possible expulsion of a member in that member's presence."

"Quite right, matey," intruded a thick voice from the armchair. "All in favour say 'aye'."

"Do you suggest," asked the chairman, "that the member be requested to leave or, if necessary, be removed from the meeting?"

"Out of consideration for the feelings of the member, I do, sir."

As the chairman silently debated this proposition, the defence took a hand.

"Although I appreciate that the motion has not been and may not be seconded, Mr. Chairman, I must point out that there is nothing in the rules of the club which debars a financial member from being present at any general meeting no matter what the subject under discussion may be. It would, in my view, be unconstitutional and therefore improper for the member to be asked to leave."

The cases for and against thus stated, the meeting pulsated in heated debate for half an hour. No solution had been reached when a loud snore came from the armchair. There is a school of thought that if you avoid a problem long enough it will solve itself. The chairman was a member of that school. He ruled that there was now no need to consider the issue of principle any further since the member concerned was, while still present at the meeting, beyond consciousness of the nature and content of the proceedings. He proposed therefore that they should resume examination of the case; and, with a few dissentient murmurs, the tides of procedural battle receded.

The future of Bessie as a member of the club occupied the members for the next two hours. The rules required the votes of two-thirds of the members present to keep him in. When the debate was closed and the stewards handed round voting papers, a second point arose. Was Bessie entitled to vote on the motion for his own expulsion or was he not? This sparked off another half hour of divided counsel which came to an end when someone pointed out that an accused did not normally vote with the jury. So Bessie was not consulted, no one apparently taking heed of the possibility that he might not, anyway, wish to remain a member.

Bessie stayed in the fold by one vote. The old heads wagged and forecast that the club was doomed if it condoned, nay encouraged, such improper behaviour. And the young ones breathed sighs of relief to think that they could still have the best of two worlds.

Bessie slept on and the steward woke him, bearded and stiff, next morning. No one knew whether he was aware how close he had gone to the guillotine; but, at the club's next annual ball, Bessie turned up alone.

Bessie was one kind of club character. The planter was another. Like most planters, he was intolerant of young new-broom civil servants with little experience and fewer brains. When I first met him in the club, he abruptly bade me sit down. I could see I was for it as he reached across the table and poured himself a generous whisky.

His eye was in the fading sun and his mind was caught in the web of the past. My presence was incidental to his reflections and my interventions were waved aside as though a dog had somehow contradicted his master. I picked up the decanter. It had not been offered to me.

"Sorry," he said, "but you know what it is when you have lived alone, as I have here, for forty years. You tend to forget the social things. Of course, I must say," he added, "that the Tongan too is not what he used to be. He's become soft on white bread, corned beef and Australian gin. I remember when I first came here we had overseas ships calling at Nuku'alofa. Ha'apai and Vava'u and even some of the smaller islands. They sent 15,000 cases of bananas from Ha'apai alone each ship and Tongan oranges and pineapples were the best in the Pacific. The people knew their limitations and if they were a bit too pleased with themselves in some ways, perhaps they had reason to be. They had at least achieved survival as the last remaining independent Polynesian kingdom in the Pacific. The only thing they ever seriously quarrelled about was their religion and those darned half-baked missionaries are to blame for that. And look at the clothes they piled on these children of nature. Told 'em it was indecent to display their bodies for God and man to see. Gave 'em influenza and tuberculosis as a result. It was solemnly put in the law—and is still there for that matter—that no Tongan might be seen in a town without a shirt on his back. If he was, he was haled before the courts. That's now got so much under their brown skins that the men are namby-pambies and the women are prudes. A couple of these so-called agriculturalists went to Tahiti recently to learn all about growing vanilla. Sweated about the fields going through shirt after shirt. The Tahitians thought they were crazy, but would those Tongans work without their shirts? Not on your life!"

The planter downed half of his whisky.

"Now there are no bananas from Ha'apai and, of course, no ships.* The citrus in Vava'u has all the diseases in the book and the canning factory is going out of business. It's no use trying to sell new ideas and new crops to the people because they just won't do anything about them while the price of copra is high."

He pronounced it "cobra". In the past, the English "b" and "p" were both spoken as a "b" in Tongan. Habit so conquered the old settlers that they followed suit in English.

"And none of the young fellers of today really know the customs and traditions of their past."

The planter was warming to his theme. "When I first came here, no Tongan ever came to town without wearing his *ta'ovala*. If a chief went by, each one of them got down on his haunches and sat

* Bananas are now being shipped again from Ha'apai.

cross-legged by the side of the road until the chief had passed. They don't do that now. All the chief gets, if he is lucky, is a cock-eyed version of an army salute. And in the normal course of events, Tongans did not pass by the Palace. It's sacred ground there still, but it really was *tapu* in the past. If a man had to bring a load of wood or food to the Palace, he hopped off his cart before he got anywhere near, and crept into the grounds on his knees. They were content too with what they had. Now they roam around in trousers, cut copra when they feel like it and go to the pictures every night. A boy came down to Nuku'alofa from Ha'afeva to work in one of the stores. When he went back to his island for a holiday a year later, his father asked him what he had got while working in the gold-starred big city. He was proudly shown a wristlet watch.

" 'That's no good!' said his father. 'You better go back again. Everyone else who went to the stores from here got himself a motor cycle or a good house or a wife, as well as a watch. You've wasted your time!'

"Cotton-wool Tongans, that's what they are now, living in half-pie wooden houses and grown sleek and bone lazy."

The planter paused to swallow and added reluctantly. "But still, I suppose they'll survive. They have unity and a supreme belief in themselves and the likes of you and me are only appendages in their way of life. They have an insatiable urge to learn from us. As soon as they have done so, or think they have, we shall be cast off like a lizard's skin and they will muddle on in their own way just as they want to. And nothing I have done"—he became categoric and severe in the glow of the whisky—"or you, young man, will be able to do, can change that. So don't get away with the idea that you can move things in your way in Tonga. You'll get so far and then you'll find yourself up against a brick wall. And just as you're about to bash your impatient young head against it, they'll intrude a feather pillow. So you'll come down to earth gently—but you'll come down just the same."

The planter was in danger of mixing his metaphors; but his meaning was clear, I recalled, as we sat down to dinner a week later. The meal was cooked and served impeccably by a

Tongan servant who prided himself on his acquired name of Mozart. This was a touch of the planter's whimsy; but the extent of it only became apparent months later when I discovered his affection for the music of Joseph Haydn—the master who came to be overshadowed by his greater pupil, Mozart.

22 The Ordeal of Tin Can Island

AWAY to the north-west of Ha'apai and 400 miles from Nuku'alofa lies the most remote island to fly the red cross of the Tongan flag. You get a glimpse of it as you sail on the fringe of Tongan waters from Samoa to Fiji. A stark and lonely island, 3½ miles long by 3 miles wide, it is, like Pitcairn, a maritime whistle-stop. For Niuafo'ou, as the Friendly Islanders call it, is the island of the Tin Can Mail.

It was an Englishman, Charles Stuart Ramsay, who conceived the idea of a tin can mail service while he was running a trading post there in the years before the second world war. Like that of Niue, the coastline of Niuafo'ou is sheer and rocky. There is no natural harbour and no reef to protect the island's frail canoes from the Pacific rollers which pound ceaselessly shorewards. Many canoes were lost when they went out to collect mail and supplies from passing ships. Others were damaged as they put into the bleak landing at Angaha. Ramsay—Lamisi, to give the Tongan version of his name—was both writer and reader. For him, isolation was one thing, ignorance another; and he relied on these infrequent mails to bring in letters and books and to take away his own correspondence to the world beyond Niuafo'ou. The occasional loss of mail bore heavily on Ramsay as he pondered what could be done about it. When, later, he came to write his story, this is how he recalled the beginnings of his Tin Can Mail service:

"One day I was watching some natives making their way down to the rocks with their buoyant swimming poles of *fau* wood to go fishing. A heavy swell was running and I wondered how they would get into the water. After a few minutes of watching the waves as they roared in, the natives suddenly seized their poles, threw them into the backwash and immediately followed. I lost sight of the men in the surging white foam, but soon they appeared a little distance out, where they again secured their wooden floats.

"The towering white crest of the close following wave imminently threatened the natives with destruction on the rocks and I held my breath. There was a flashing glimpse of strong brown arms, and the poles sailed into the air over the white crest. Then the swimmers dived beneath the roaring monster in front of them, to reappear beyond the danger zone of the breaking waves.

"I said to myself, 'Now, why can't I do that?' "

So Ramsay began his swims to passing steamers. He was a slightly built man and not a naturally powerful swimmer. Yet he went out in the roughest seas for his precious books and letters. It was a two-mile swim on each occasion, but there were more daunting hazards than the need for endurance. He faced possible death every time he plunged into the turbulent sea. An error in timing his jump between a crashing roller and the swift ebb that followed would have meant his being dashed against the razor-sharp rocks. Soon Ramsay and his assistants developed a routine for preparing and handling the mail they took with them. The outward mail was made up ashore into several parcels, wrapped in oiled water-proof paper, and tied to the ends of sticks about three feet in length. Two or three Tongans swam with Ramsay to the ships, each with a stick to which a parcel of mail had been tied. Their bodies were supported by the long *fau* poles. When the swimmers reached the ship, the mail parcels were placed in buckets lowered from the deck of the steamer. Then large sealed biscuit tins, containing the inward mail and literature were put down or tossed overboard to the swimming mailmen, who took them the long mile back to Niuafo'ou.

There were times when Ramsay did come close to death. Once, his Tongan companion was seized and fatally injured by a marauding shark. Ramsay struggled ashore exhausted after a vain attempt to save his fellow swimmer's life. Another time he swam out in the dark through mountainous waves to meet the first *Tofua*, an old coal-burner long since scrapped. He arrived to see the lights of the steamer disappearing into the night. This time Ramsay's strength failed and he struggled desperately against the undertow as he neared the shore. It was a whim of providence that he was carried by a sudden counter-current close to the Angaha landing, where his limp body was dragged to safety through the broiling breakers.

Then there was the night when the ship's captain, thinking that Ramsay and his assistant, Biutau, were well clear of the hull, signalled the engine room to get underway. The vessel swung around and Biutau, caught in the ship's wake and about to be mangled by the whirling propellers, shouted to Ramsay, "Lamisi, *tokoni mai—teu mate!* (Ramsay, help me, or I shall die!)" Ramsay described what then followed.

"Biutau was helpless to save himself, and heaven only knows what I thought I could do to save him, but flinging aside my swimming pole, I instinctively struck out for him with all my speed. I yelled with all the strength of my lungs, 'Ahoy, the bridge! For God's sake, stop the engines.'

"When I reached Biutau, the stern was almost upon us. In spite of our frenzied efforts to escape, it swept, like a juggernaut, inexorably nearer. Then, in a panic of fear, we felt the drag of the propellers and foresaw ourselves being sucked to an awful death, gashed and ripped by the thrashing blades.

" 'Let the tin go!' I gasped to Biutau, as we fought the deadly undertow. The mail tin, released from our hands, was pulled past our shoulders to the propellers and sucked down out of sight.

"Then there came one of the grandest sounds that has ever reached my ears, the engine room telegraph signalling—STOP! Only a second saved us. As the impetus of the steamer carried her overhanging stern like a roof above our heads, the blades of the motionless propellers actually bumped us in the dark!"

The Chief Officer, about to signal full speed ahead, which would have spelled a horrible mutilated death to the two swimmers, had miraculously heard Ramsay's faint cries.

The Tin Can Mail service was interrupted during the war and when the island was evacuated in 1946. Now it is in operation again, more sophisticated perhaps but less picturesque. The American Matson Line cruise ships pass by Niuafo'ou on their monthly voyages from Suva to Pago Pago. Ramsay has long since left for New Zealand and the swimmers are no more. Instead, the mail men, in T-shirts and base-ball caps with "Monterey" or "Mariposa" stamped in black letters on the peaks, come out in canoes with their large biscuit tins of mail. These contain the stamped letters posted by passengers on the previous voyage. They leave Niuafo'ou a month later for delivery all over the world. The inward mail is lowered to the waiting canoes. Some sacks of potatoes may follow, then a blast of the ship's siren and the Tin Can Mail service goes into retreat for another four weeks . . .

The Tin Can Mail is only one part of the story of Niuafo'ou. The heart of it lies in the nature of the island itself and its active volcanic history. The summit of the central crater is about 600 feet above sea level. The top of what is now the central cone blew off many centuries ago. It is filled by a large lake fed by hot springs. The size of Niuafo'ou is officially put at nineteen square miles: of these the lake accounts for six. The rest of the island is a near-circular crust of fertile land fringing the main crater. From the air, it resembles a large doughnut. Locked within the high volcanic rim is a series of smaller craters and crater lakes. Within the lakes are more volcanic upthrusts, within which in turn are yet more lakes. There are lakes within volcanoes within lakes within volcanoes within lakes within one huge island volcano. There are more than thirty points of volcanic eruption; and life for the people of Niuafo'ou has been one of destroyed villages, ruined crops and loss of life and property. It may seem strange that the island remained inhabited; but the deep-rooted sentimental attachment of the Polynesian to his own tribal or family land is the reason.

One inky night in August 1886, an earthquake shook the island with a gentle swaying motion. Smaller shocks followed. Then with a tremendous roar, a volcanic eruption mushroomed up 3,000 feet above the lake and the earthquake ceased. A violent thunderstorm followed and lightning struck in many places. A blizzard of black dust and sand weighed down the houses and vegetation. Spasmodic eruptions like geysers occurred during the next eighteen days and clouds of dust dimmed the light of day. In July 1929, there was another nightmare of erupting violence which destroyed the village of Futu. The people were awakened by a low rumbling as fire broke out on the hillside to the south-east. The aged, the sick and young children were evacuated to the high ground of the island's circular ridge. From three vents in a fracture that opened in the crust of the earth, molten rock descended on Futu. Soon the abandoned buildings had been consumed by fire and buried under floods of heavy basaltic lava. Pouring into the ocean, the hot flows killed fish, sent up clouds of steam and heaped mountains of black sand on the rocky coast.

In 1935 and 1936, the violence returned again. Ahau, the most fertile part of the island, was destroyed, the village of Petani threatened. In 1943, another eruption wrecked houses and ruined food crops. Then, three years later, came the great ordeal of the people of Niuafo'ou when their island was all but submerged by the savage onslaught which struck it.

The day's work was over and it was night. The hurricane lamps shone in the faces of the men of Angaha as they sat drinking *kava*. Stone cracked on stone as the girl crushed the dry root for the next mixing. It was the timeless custom of this village and every village; the nightly gossip of the *faikava*, the scandals and speculations of tongues relaxed by the ceremonial brown liquid. Old men, withered in body but yet fresh in mind, basked in the reflective talk of their age; while the young listened and learned of love and sport and how to win in both.

A warm, friendly evening at seven o'clock on the night of the 9th September, 1946—like many another before and since.

From the distance, faintly, came a rumble as of thunder. Ears lifted to the west whence the sound had come. Abruptly the chatter was stilled. Inside was silence but for the lamps which hissed as they swung back and forth from the hooks on the beam. A chill ripple ran through the hut. *Kava* swilled over the broad lip of the wooden bowl.

Throughout the night, Niuafo'ou shivered and creaked, giving to all that claustrophobic fear for life and property peculiar to earthquakes and hurricanes. The dawn came bleak and comfortless. Over the island's smouldering ruin hung a film of steam pierced here and there by spirals of blue smoke from lava fires which still burned in the undergrowth. The island itself was a scarred and battered shell; and the principal town of Angaha had all but vanished.

Wireless telegraphy had been installed on Niuafo'ou in 1930. The operator in 1946 was S. M. Manu, who had the presence of mind to keep a diary of the terrible events which then took place. These are some extracts from what he wrote:

> *9.9.46: 8.15 p.m.* Copra Inspector called from verandah that something queer is seen. Ran out and to my horror the western approach to Angaha is all in flames and smoke thousands of feet high. Can hear clearly big trees and coconut trees snap when waves of lava reach them. My estimate as well as others, was that the fire is now at the end of Angaha—almost at the hospital. Abandoned everything and started for the hill. Fire seems to cover all western approaches from the sea up to village of Esia, so ran towards Sapa'ata village. Joined by teacher outside the station. We started at a slow trot, hoping that the fire will not reach the town. Stopped near end of Angaha and had another look at the eruption. A big flash of lightning ran from the sea from a north-easterly direction to about 100 yards from where we stood accompanied by an eruption from the sea, directly in front of Dougal Quensell's property. We now ran for our lives. When we reached Sapa'ata, the fire looked as if it is where we stood not three minutes ago. People running to the hill, a whole mass of men, women, children and animals, all struggling together. Whole place brightly lit by fire. Moon obscured by fire and smoke. Piu was considered unsafe as it was too close to Angaha, so all run up to Mokotu point, about a mile from Angaha. Could see from Mokotu fire raging at Angaha. Wireless masts still stand in midst of fire. After about an hour, we went to Piu where we saw the destruction of the wireless station, Government offices and quarters by two craters, one about ten yards from our kitchen and one beside Fotofili's house about twenty yards from the office. There are other small openings at various places at Angaha which spout fire but not lava.
>
> *11 p.m.* Light rain mixed with sand came down. For the first

time I realised that I have nothing except the shirt and *vala* which I wore, my only things saved together with office and safe keys and a tuning fork. All other things lost. Later found out that I shared this misfortune with Magistrate, Police officers, Assistant Operator Robert Tupou, Copra Inspector, storekeepers and others. People now start building shelters. Back from Piu, wet, found no place to sleep so went down to Fata'ulua village and spent an uncomfortable night at the house of Ha'angana's father-in-law.

10.9.46: 10 a.m. In addition to three craters at Angaha, about nine others are found from 'Utu Palapu to 'Alelea, the crater at the outskirts of Angaha, about a hundred yards from dispensary. All these craters are in line along the beach. 'Alelea erupted towards the sea, and along the beach to the dispensary. Pule erupted in the sea, and runs in a westerly direction, covering the landing place and stopping. There is an opening of about twenty or thirty yards between them. Lava has extended right out to sea; whether it will stay or not will depend on the durability of the lava to stand the force of the waves. The new beach is covered by a kind of rough black sand, and boats can now land there with ease.

11.9.46: 11.30 a.m. About 11 a.m. we managed to pull out the small safe from Government office. We broke this safe and recovered £34 in silver. All paper currency burned. Unable to pull out the big safe as it was surrounded by hot thick lava and covered by hot rough black sand from 'Alelea crater, a few yards away. This crater erupted strongly again last night, and by morning a big hill had formed there, about two or three hundred feet high. Today with a long stick I wrote an SOS beside it about where the meteorological hut had stood. An aircraft passed well to the north at noon. Going westerly, might be from Samoa to Fiji. 'Alelea crater has stopped erupting but makes an occasional roar like that of a lion, so that people near it run for their lives. All wireless gear destroyed by lava together with two big clocks and one alarm clock. Wireless masts covered by thick layer of lava, which is about as thick as old Quensell's fence. Wireless room also shared same fate. Living quarters worse as they were too* close to crater; lava covered up to half of cement tank. No one ever dreamed that we were living and working between two huge craters. If all the craters erupted at the same time, I, Ha'angana, Mr. Wolfgramm and teacher (the last to leave Angaha) will be trapped inside wireless room and no hope of escape. Luckily, and for some unknown reason, the Angaha craters seem to wait until we were all cleared from the danger area, then they let everything go. If the eruption occurred between midnight and 6 a.m. there will be many loss of life. Although the material damage caused by the eruption is too great, we thank the Almighty God from the bottom of our hearts that through his kindness and unending love, no lives were lost.

A harrowing ten days followed as the people of Niuafo'ou tried to bring a semblance of order out of chaos. Six days after the disaster, an American Catalina circled over the still steaming island and half an hour later a radio signal to Nuku'alofa gave the first news of what had happened. Plans for immediate relief operations were soon under way and a decision later reached that everyone should be evacuated. On the 21st December, the Union Steam Ship Company's other islands vessel *Matua* arrived to take them all to Nuku'alofa. Nature had at last won its battle with the resilience of man.

Most of the 1,300 people settled on the island of 'Eua, rich, fertile and hospitable, lying off the southern coast of Tongatapu. There in exile they maintained the framework and ties of their old tribal identities: "The Niua people"—at once both strangers and brothers—to the men of 'Eua.

The problems of re-settlement continue and twenty years after the evacuation of Niuafo'ou, an Evacuation Committee still meets to arrange the occasional cutting and shipment of copra from the island and to administer the funds derived from its sale. Permanent habitation of Niuafo'ou remained officially forbidden until 1958.

* The Tongan word *fu'u* has to make do for both "very" and "too" in English, the latter in the sense of, for example, "too tired to go further". When he learns English, the Tongan finds it difficult to distinguish between the English language usage of "very" and "too". He frequently makes this quaint but not unattractive mistake.

During the preceding ten years, pressure had grown from the Niuafo'ou people for permission to return to their ancestral home—to their ruined houses and gardens, the trees and birds and fish, the grave-yards of their forebears, and, above all, to resume the struggle for survival against the forces of nature. To permit them to return was an agonising decision for Queen Salote and her Ministers to take.

In September 1958, the first party of 200 was allowed to go back to their devastated island—an occasion of such sentimental significance that it is not easy for non-Polynesians fully to comprehend. Their island has a history of nine major eruptions in the past century. On each occasion, villages, paths, houses and gardens had been destroyed. Yet, they are there today, fearful but happy, no longer landless exiles, but back with their ancestors. The spirits of the dead have ceased to wander forlorn on the night winds of Niuafo'ou.

The story has a short postscript. The islanders of Niuafo'ou entertain a belief that the natural disasters which have befallen their homeland have been sent as punishment for wrong done or evil wrought by the chiefs of the island. Whether or not this is a Polynesian example of blame transference, the chiefly administrators of Tin Can Island are likely to continue to be as benevolent as human frailties permit.

Fijian chiefs and their wives are received by His Majesty King Taufaʻahau Tupou IV at the Palace. Two of the King's *matapule* are seated at the right

King Taufaʻahau Tupou IV and Queen Mataʻaho lead the procession of mourners from the Palace to the Royal Tombs. They are walking on a carpet of *tapa* cloth. At the left of the tree is Queen Mata'aho's mother, Heuifanga. In the centre of the women holding the mats is Leafa, the Samoan widow of a former Deputy Premier and Noble, Havea Tuʻihaʻateiho

The bier approaches the Royal Tombs

The women raise a screen of mats as the vault containing the body of Queen Salote's husband is opened

23 Diversions of a Government Secretary

THE casual visitor had a glossy-magazine conception of what working in Tonga was really like. "I suppose you have very little to do," they said, "since most problems must solve themselves—relaxing, easygoing, music, dances, feasts, the rustle of the palm trees . . . Work? Surely not!" We used to smile as indulgently as we could.

The newcomer to official responsibility in Tonga was greeted with some unusual aspects of administrative organisation and procedure. He needed a period of adjustment to them. A daily-wage labourer in the Public Works Department would ask for a rise and, without comment, the request would be sent in to the Premier's office for consideration. With some exceptions, those concerned were coy about committing themselves on paper with a positive recommendation on a matter of this kind. There was some native sense in this. The cousin of the suppliant might be the Minister's typist and the messenger his nephew. Frankness and objectivity on paper were not therefore without problems. So was the preservation of official secrecy in the conduct of the affairs of state. The person affected by an administrative decision might be the last to hear about it. Confidential discussions could not be relied upon. In deciding a course of action after they had taken place, it was sensible to assume that their content was generally known. To do otherwise would have been naïve.

The resolution of an apparently straightforward proposition took time—sometimes because it was not, in the Tongan context, necessarily straightforward at all. Attitudes had to be re-thought. Concepts of logic, right and wrong, decision, administration—as learned elsewhere—did not necessarily apply. Words took on a new and more complex meaning. The real core of a problem could be elusive. Putting things right again after misadventure bore hard on the nervous system: like the time when the technicians of the Nuku'alofa Electric Power Board were desperately trying to repair faulty generators and so get the hospital refrigerators going again and the wireless transmitter back on the air. It was Sunday morning and they were arrested by the police for a breach of the constitutional prohibition of Sunday work.

Tongan administration was not always so literal-minded. Prince Tungi took an eminently relaxed and practical view of life.

"A few years ago," he told me, "there was a sudden and apparently unaccountable shortage of timber in the Government Works Department. All enquiries within the Department failed to reveal any clue as to the whereabouts of the missing timber. Some months later it was observed that many of the departmental labourers had built themselves brand-new European-style wooden houses. We didn't want to prosecute them because if they had all gone to gaol we should have had no one to carry out the labour required.

"So we said to them nicely: 'Look, we know you've been naughty and taken all the Government timber, but if you promise to pay for it we'll say no more about it.'

"Then they all looked self-righteous and said that each had given the other permission and of course they had intended to pay for it all the time.

"So we said don't do it again, ordered some more timber, they all paid up, and work in the Department went on happily without interruption."

In the outlying districts, authority coalesced in the shape of the local governor. There were two, one in Ha'apai and one in Vava'u. In the case of both, the word of Nuku'alofa was essential to act or decision. This tended to dampen the initiative of the local people, who occasionally complained among themselves about the appointment of Tongans to these key posts who, they said, had rank but no other qualification. This may or may not have been so, but the fact was that neither the profoundly loyal people of Ha'apai nor the turbulent Irishmen of Vava'u would tolerate a commoner, no matter how competent, as their governor. So the malcontents grumbled silently while life and the administration of public business went on as best it could. Periodic visits by Ministers or heads of departments served temporarily to stimulate local energies; but after their ships had faded into the horizon lassitude seemed to descend over the coconut palms again.

The Governor of Ha'apai took comfort in the approval of Nuku'alofa to his actions. One afternoon the incensed voice of the Government Dentist came on my telephone:

"Heh, I'm in need of help. Can I have some?"

"It all depends on . . ."

"Yes, I know all that stuff, but I've just had a telegram from Ha'apai. The silly clots are mucking up one of my blokes."

The dentist was a forthright New Zealander and his language became unprintable. The operator's switch clicked out from the line as she turned off the tap of gossip.

"I sent up one of my dental assistants to Ha'apai to relieve there while the local chap is on tour. And now I get this damn silly telegram. I'll read it to you.

" 'To Government Dentist, Nuku'alofa stop Tapealava arrived yesterday stop Mapa away on tour with key stop Please see Premier to give authority to open dental room with hammer urgently stop Governor Ha'apai.' Well, what do you think of that?"

"I think," I replied, "firstly, that your Mapa is a bit of a dolt for rushing off round the Pacific with the key of the dental room in his pocket. However," I added hastily, "the room had better be opened. I suppose we can assume that there is a hammer in Ha'apai unless the only one is locked up with the dental equipment."

This was no way to placate an irate dentist. I hastened to assure him that authority to resolve this impasse would promptly be telegraphed to Ha'apai. I had a pang of remorse at being instrumental in putting an end to the unexpected relief of the Ha'apai Tongans who had in the past few days retreated from the closed doors of the dental room.

In due time, the door was breached by the Governor with a telegram of Prime Ministerial authority in one hand and a hammer in the other. A resentful politician later wrote seeking my deportation for taking too much unto myself. He would, I suppose, have preferred me to submit the problem of the locked dental door for consideration by the Cabinet.

Official correspondence was often disconcerting, always colourful, and never dull. There were the notes of Havili the milkman and his request for "£1 for whale", and the endearing periodic pleas of filing clerk Vaetangitau.

During much of the period between 1953 and 1956, the only means of sending mail to the outside world was on the occasion of the four-weekly call at Nuku'alofa by the *Tofua*. There was an infrequent copra ship; an RNZAF Sunderland flew in from time to time from Lauthala Bay in Suva; and latterly, we had a monthly charter flying boat service operated by Tasman Empire Airways Ltd. The *Tofua* put in at seven a.m. every fourth Monday. This was Mail Day—a known, calendar-ringed date—quite distinct from other fortuitous occasions. It was a hectic time because commercial firms, missions, government departments and families all wanted to collect their stack of inward mail at the earliest possible moment, get it answered and the replies posted before the outward mail closed again. Passions ran high and complaints were legion whenever there was delay in the sorting room.

The Chief Postmaster, one Lorne Denny, was a benevolent soul who believed in doing his best on these occasions. He was of New Zealand origin, born in Tonga and he was sympathetic to public sentiment. Flexibility was his watchword as he wrestled to bring order and service out of the fervour of Mail Day. He did not, of course, succeed, but the public was tolerably satisfied with his attempts. He became ill in the process and retired to Auckland. His successor, a Dutchman from Indonesia, was unsuited by temperament to work in Tonga. He introduced a new order. This provided for the outward mail to be closed and bagged before the sacks of inward mail were opened and sorted in the Post Office, during which time there was to be no counter service. Not unexpectedly, this provoked an outcry. The new Chief Postmaster stood firm: "I have neither room nor staff to deal with inward and outward mail and stamp sales at the same time. We cannot continue if we are to be asked to do so."

Chief Postmasters were scarce round about 1955—at least, in Tonga they were. The chips were down and officialdom closed its ears to public pleas for a time. Then the captain of the Government ketch *Hifofua* took a hand. He was a no-nonsense heavyweight from Hamburg who had gone to Australia before the second world war. There he had acquired facility in earthy English suitable for situations such as this. He first taught me that ridicule is the ultimate weapon against political or official ineptitude. Whenever he became really cross, he composed a bit of doggerel which was selectively circulated in sufficient quantity to get results. He did so on this occasion. The tactful note from Vaeatangitau said, "Just for your sparetime reading," as I picked up the verses from my desk one morning:

Tonga's an island Kingdom
In the sparkling southern seas
Where the sun makes play with the wavelets
And tempers a south-east breeze.

Conditions are restful and easy
Except when you deal with the post
You'll find the office not open
Just when you're wanting it most.

When the mail comes in *ex Tofua*
She arrives very soon after seven,
You can't buy a stamp or post letters
Till the clock's striking half past eleven.

The incoming mail's to be sorted
The outgoing mail put in sacks
That's what we're told is the reason
For a service that everyone lacks.

The Chiefest of all the Postmasters
Is certainly doing his level
To establish a bureaucrats' heaven
The public can go to the devil.

So give us back our Lornie
Who got all the business done
With a minimum of bullshit
And a maximum of fun.

Spokeshave

Lornie did not come back; but the new man was beaten. Shortly thereafter it became possible, once again, to buy stamps and post outgoing letters while the inward mail was being sorted.

This was the opening gambit of an appeal by the magistrates for a salary increase:

> We humbly pray Her Gracious Majesty and Honourable Privy Councillors to listen to the singing of wee tiny birds from a nest of anxiety which hangs from an indigenous tree in your Kingdom. No doubt they are singing what is but a familiar tune; and if the singing may not be thought melodious, it is that some of the voices are pitiable and in a sorry plight. And yet the tune may yet be idyllic, if Her Majesty graciously consents to harmonize with the singers.
>
> We are public servants in the Courts of your Kingdom and for the reasons set out below, we beseech an increase in our salary scales . . .

Then followed a highly coloured and emotive appeal for release from financial thraldom, which seemed to make little impact on the Salaries Commissioner.

We advertised for a gardener at 'Atalanga, the official residence owned by the Government of Tonga at Auckland where the Queen stayed during her periodic visits. The Tongan students awarded scholarships to study in New Zealand also lived there in a neighbouring house. The world beyond the foam-capped reefs of the Pacific exerted an irresistible appeal upon the youth of all its islands and the young men of Tonga were no exception. The file about stowaways to Fiji never had time to gather dust. The opportunity for employment in New Zealand under the wing of the Tonga Government accordingly brought in a large field of applicants, each of whom produced the most compelling reasons why his appointment was essential to the future well-being of the Government, the people and the gardens of ‘Atalanga. Perhaps the best bit of penmanship wound up in this way:

> I shall be much exceedingly pleased to say that I am quite agreeable for the salary, accommodation, food and uniform in connection with the position in question. I wish to let you know that, if ever I am chosen for the job, I shall be working, sweating and wet at all times.

Sadly, he ended up second in the race and thus never had the opportunity to put his expressed intentions into practice. He would have been unusual if he had.

Then there were the two carpenters of the Tonga Copra Board who decided to tender for a job to be done for their employers! They wrote this letter, in English, to the district manager:

> The Right Honourable Mister Kuli Kaho
> Supervising Manager,
> Ha‘apai District
> Tonga Copra Board
> Pangai, Ha‘apai
>
> Dear Sir;
>
> We, the undersigned, being one George Brown and Viliame Konga‘ika have the privilege of submitting our bid for the expected work contemplated to be done to the living quarters of the Ha‘apai Superintendent, Tonga Copra Board. Said work includes in our understanding the raising of said house to the height of four feet, replacing the plates beneath the house and forming new cement foundation blocks for the foundation of the said house.
>
> We have considered carefully the work and have arrived at the value of £200.0.0 with materials being furnished and a given time period of four weeks to complete said work. We feel certain that if given the opportunity to perform the said work, your satisfaction can be assured.
>
> As for qualifications, both of us have had considerable experience in carpentry work, both being presently employed as

carpenters for the Ha'apai District, Tonga Copra Board. The said Viliame has worked for the Tonga Public Works Department, Ha'apai District for eight months and has for the past six months been employed by the Ha'apai District, Tonga Copra Board as a carpenter. The said George Brown has worked at private building and has this year been employed by the Ha'apai District, Tonga Copra Board.

Both of the above have worked as Missionaries in the Church of Jesus Christ of Latter Day Saints and have done a very highly class work in that organisation. George worked for three years and three months, and Viliame worked for three years and six months. This work is of a volunteer nature with no pay whatsoever being tendered or sought. Their reliability has thus been sustained in most every phase sought by those seeking workers for a work of this nature.

Hoping that this bid meets with the fair approval of the Honourable Superintendent, Ha'apai District, Tonga Copra Board, we remain

Respectfully yours,
V. Konga'ika
S. Palauni.

P.S. Our value of £200, was reached after careful deliberation, but we are willing to fluctuate it, so that we will be below the lowest bid by £5 no matter what the lowest bid is.

One day shortly before the Royal Visit, I opened a file entitled "Nuku'alofa War Memorial". In it was a letter in Tongan addressed to the Premier. The translation read as follows:

In view of the coming visit of Her Britannic Majesty Queen Elizabeth, it is a matter of deep concern to me that my name has never been inscribed on the Nuku'alofa War Memorial.

My registered name in the Forces was S. TU'INUKUAFE No. 60798 L.C.N.Z.

I joined up in New Zealand early in 1918 and went to Palestine. I am a Tongan subject.

Siaosi Tu'inukuafe

I read through this plea somewhat cursorily; and with, I thought, more weighty matters on hand at the time, minuted back the papers a little testily:

Chief Clerk,

Please reply to page 38 saying that a war memorial, as the name implies, is erected in memory of those who *died* in the war concerned. The petitioner's name is absent from the list since he is apparently still alive.

K.R.B.

That seemed to be that.

The file reappeared next day. The chief clerk pointed out politely but firmly that I had perhaps overlooked the fact that the list of names on the memorial included *all* men from Tonga who had served in both wars and not merely those who had not survived. In the circumstances, did I feel that he should proceed with the reply on the lines indicated?

That afternoon I gave the memorial a closer study than I had hitherto accorded it. The chief clerk was correct. Queen Elizabeth was to pay homage to the dead by laying a wreath on the memorial shortly after her arrival in Nuku'alofa. Beneath the statue of an infantryman with reversed rifle were lists of names from both world wars. They included many whom I knew to be still very much alive. Here was a matter of some delicacy: but nothing could be done about it.

A fortnight later Queen Elizabeth laid the wreath to the memory of the Tongan fallen. Her Majesty then inspected a guard of returned servicemen who had witnessed this royal commemoration of their honourable decease on the field of battle.

24 The Shadow of Royal Death

CONTINUITY of leadership marks the destiny of nations and people. From the nature of it stems national pride, thence a sense of identity and stability. The people of Tonga have been blessed in this respect. King George Tupou I had laid the foundations of a modern state during a reign of over forty-seven years. As the Queen approached her sixty-fifth birthday on the 13th March, 1965, her people also looked forward to celebrating the longest-ever reign of a Tongan sovereign.

Both the Queen's pleasure and her people's joy were coloured by unspoken foreboding. For years the Queen had silently suffered the torment of diabetes; and it had been her practice to travel by sea each year to Auckland for medical care. There she stayed simply and without fuss at the residence bought for her in 1954 by her Government. As the disease had grown in severity, so the Queen had felt obliged to curtail her public engagements. Breaking a tradition begun by George Tupou I, carried on by George Tupou II and followed throughout most of her long reign, Queen Salote no longer felt able to open or close the annual session of the Legislative Assembly. As her strength began to ebb, the Queen could not manage the staircase of the Royal Palace; and although Crown Prince Tungi wished to instal a lift for his mother, she preferred to move out of the Palace to the foreshore home of her second son, Prince Tu'ipelehake. She began to lose weight. Her resplendent hair, so long her crowning joy, began to turn from grey to white. Then the trade winds whispered the diagnosis of cancer to the rusty fringes of the palm leaves; and old men sat at night round the *kava* bowls, their voices stilled, until the Polynesian sky glowed amber with the new day. And their Queen moved less and less from her room.

The 30th July, 1965, was set aside for the celebration of the

Queen's long reign. At Nuku'alofa, a twenty-one-gun salute was fired and five school bands led 10,000 children in a parade over two miles long through the Palace grounds. Queen Salote was the epitome of all grandmothers. She loved and indulged her own grandchildren. She was never happier than when sharing the happiness of children. Their tributes to her, in return, never failed to touch her deeply; and she knew what the circumstances of the next occasion would be as she watched the parade from her armchair on the Palace verandah. In her hand was a message, delivered that morning by A. C. Reid, the British Commissioner and Consul, from Queen Elizabeth in London:

> I have learned with great pleasure that your long and distinguished reign, having now surpassed in length that of your illustrious predecessor, King George I, is being celebrated today in Tonga. This is indeed a proud day in the history of the Kingdom. My husband and I have happy memories of our visit to Tonga in 1953 and send you our warmest good wishes on this historic occasion.
>
> ELIZABETH R.

And so three months of ordeal and endurance went by. Then a final attempt was made. At the end of October came news that Queen Elizabeth had offered to arrange for an aircraft of the Royal Air Force to fly the Queen of Tonga to New Zealand for medical treatment. This followed the granting of an audience by Queen Elizabeth to Crown Prince Tungi three days before, in London.

Accompanied by her Deputy Premier and second son, Prince Tu'ipelehake, his wife Princess Melenaite and her ADC Ngalumoetutulu Kaliniuvalu, the Queen left Fua'amotu Airport for the last time on the 4th November. The party travelled to Nadi International Airport in Fiji by an RAF Argosy aircraft and changed there into a Britannia for the flight to Auckland. It had been a sombre departure. There were no farewell ceremonies and the airport was closed off. Yet throughout the length of the thirteen mile route from Nuku'alofa were groups of the Queen's subjects gathered to see their Sovereign depart and to pray for her safe return. At one village, the people had built an archway across the road and spread mats and *tapa* cloth on the road from one end of the village to the other. The Queen smiled as she boarded the aircraft—not the London smile of joy-giving and joy-receiving; but the sweet sad smile of farewell. For no one in Tonga was to see her again, alive. And perhaps she knew, as she departed on that last journey.

Queen Salote had been created a DBE in 1932 by King George V; a GBE in 1945 by King George VI; and a GCVO at the time of the Royal Visit to Tonga in 1953. Now Queen Elizabeth bestowed a last honour: that of Dame Grand Cross of the Order of St. Michael and St. George. And so Her Majesty Queen Salote Tupou III became the first woman in history to be so distinguished. The appointment was welcomed by press and radio throughout the world. The *New Zealand Herald* reflected national response under the heading

RIGHT REGAL AWARD

The Queen has made a singularly happy gesture in appointing Queen Salote of Tonga as first Dame Grand Cross of the Order of St. Michael and St. George. Queen Salote can fairly be classed as one of the notable women of her times, not the least because of an integrity which down the years has unerringly distinguished the virtues worth preserving in an era of sweeping changes.

The world at large still knows Queen Salote by the famous smile which won the hearts of throngs in London at the time of the Coronation of Queen Elizabeth. But the peoples of all South Pacific countries have admired her, during a very lengthy reign, for many other attributes.

The Christian standards which, by precept and example, the Tongan ruler has maintained in a small group of South Sea islands could be noted by much larger and wealthier countries to their very great advantage.

Auckland takes particular pleasure in the honour awarded to Queen Salote because she has made our city her second home. Aucklanders have respected her privacy during her annual sojourns and in return have found her dignity and serenity a palliative amid the stridencies of modern life. Long and close acquaintance has served to bring enhanced respect for a very gracious lady.

When the end came, it was crushingly sudden and tragic. From Auckland, on the afternoon of Sunday the 12th December, Tu'ipelehake telephoned his brother, who, in the absence of the Queen, was Prince Regent. Their mother's condition had deteriorated suddenly. She was having difficulty in breathing and had been rushed to the Aotea Hospital. The prognosis was not good and there was cause for deep anxiety. Yet the Queen had a restful night and there was a slight improvement the following morning. As so often happens, it was to be but a brief reprieve before the end.

The Queen's nobles were summoned to the Palace. After a meeting of the Privy Council on the morning of Tuesday the 14th December, Prince Tungi and his wife Princess Mata'aho flew from Tonga to Fiji to connect with an Air New Zealand flight to Auckland next day. They will not forget the agonising hours that followed. There was an aircraft delay—at first for the morning, then for the afternoon, then into the darkness of the night, before the aircraft finally took off for New Zealand.

In her hospital bed, Queen Salote rallied to ask what delayed her elder son, her successor, the new King of Tonga and his Queen. He was not to reach her bedside in time. With Prince Tungi's aircraft still an hour out from Auckland, the Queen expired and passed to her rest at 12.15 a.m. on Thursday the 16th December, 1965. An era of Tongan history had come to an end.

In the absence of the sovereign and her two sons, the mantle of responsibility rested with Mahe 'Uli'uli Tupouniua a talented, modest commoner who had earlier become Minister of Finance. At five a.m. his telephone rang. The radio operator, his voice broken in Polynesian emotion, said "I have a telegram from Auckland for you. It is from Tungi."

Mahe paused. "Is it good news or bad news?" he asked.

"It is . . . bad news."

"Then do not read it to me. I will come to the wireless station to read it myself."

And with his eyes already dimming with unbelieving tears, Mahe went to collect the fateful cable.

Later that day, he sent this message to His Majesty King Taufa'ahu Tupou IV at Auckland:

> Her Majesty's Government, Nobles and people deeply mourn Her Majesty Queen Salote's passing and send heartfelt sympathies to Your Majesty and to members of the Royal Family. I have convened Nobles and Cabinet, have announced the Queen's death and proclaimed Your Majesty King Taufa'ahu Tupou IV in their presence.

On Friday the 17th December, 1965, the *Tonga Government Gazette* appeared in heavy black borders for the first time since the death of King George VI. It is reproduced exactly as it came out, in English and Tongan, on pp. 191–4.

As the *Tonga Chronicle* put it:

> In the words of a long forgotten Tongan poet "PUNAKAKI E FA KA OKU KEI ALAHA HONO TU'UNGA" which translated means "The flower of the pandanus has fallen, but its sweet scent still lingers on." So let it be with our beloved late Queen, Her Majesty Queen Salote Tupou III.

In Auckland, the Queen's body was taken to Government House where she lay in state. Thousands, including many Tongans resident in New Zealand, filed past to pay their last respects. On Monday the 20th December, the coffin was taken to Whenuapai Airport and flown back to Tonga by a Hercules aircraft of the Royal New Zealand Air Force. Awaiting its arrival and clad in black with the large, tattered mats of mourning, were the new King and his Queen, who had returned to Nuku'alofa two days earlier; their eldest son Crown Prince Taufa'ahau, who had flown to Tonga from school in England; and Queen Salote's other grandchildren, Pilolevu, Siuilikutapu and 'Uluvalu. Prince Tu'ipelehake and his wife Melenaite accompanied the Queen's coffin on the flight from Auckland.

TONGA GOVERNMENT GAZETTE

PUBLISHED BY AUTHORITY

No. 16 | FRIDAY 17th DECEMBER | 1965

Death of Her Majesty Queen Salote Tupou III, G.C.M.G., G.C.V.O., G.B.E.

It is with deep sorrow and profound regret, shared by the Nobles, the people and the foreign residents of Tonga, that I have to announce the most lamentable death of Her Majesty Queen Salote Tupou, which occurred at 12.15 a.m. on the 16th December, 1965, in Auckland, New Zealand.

I have been commanded to cause to be observed a period of six months mourning following the much lamented death of Her late Majesty — a Queen so greatly loved by us all.

MAHE 'ULI'ULI TUPOUNIUA,
Acting Premier.

Premier's Office,
Nuku'alofa,
16th December, 1965.

The issue of the *Tonga Government Gazette* which announced Queen Salote's death

16/246

PROCLAMATION.

In the name of His Majesty
TAUFA'AHAU TUPOU IV
King of Tonga.

By the Honourable Mahe 'Uli'uli Tupouniua,
Acting Premier of the Kingdom of Tonga.

Whereas it has pleased Almighty God to call to His mercy Her late Majesty Queen Salote Tupou III of glorious and happy memory, by whose decease the Crown of the Kingdom of Tonga is solely and rightly come to Prince Tupouto'a-Tungi, We, Mahe 'Uli'uli Tupouniua, Acting Premier; Ma'afu, Speaker of the Legislative Assembly; Salesi Manoa Havea, Minister of Police; Afu Taumoepeau, Minister without Portfolio; Vaea, the Acting Minister of Lands and of Health; Members of the Privy Council of the said Kingdom, do now hereby, with one full voice and consent of tongue and heart, publish and proclaim that the Prince Tupouto'a-Tungi is now by the death of Her late Majesty become the only lawful and rightful heir to the throne, by the Grace of God, King of the Kingdom of Tonga, to whom we do acknowledge all faith and constant obedience with all hearty and humble affection, beseeching God by Whom Kings and Queens do reign, to bless His Majesty King TAUFA'AHAU TUPOU IV with long and happy years to reign over us.

Given under my hand at Nuku'alofa, this 16th day of December in the Year of our Lord one thousand nine hundred and sixty-five.

M. E. TONGA,
Clerk to Privy Council.

GOD SAVE THE KING.

Ko e Faka'ilo 'a e Hala 'a 'Ene 'Afio ko Kuini Salote Tupou III, G.C.M.G., G.C.V.O., G.B.E.

'I he loto mamahi faka'aufulí 'oku ou fai 'a e Tohi Fanongonongó ni, pea 'oku óu lave'i pau 'oku kaungā-mamahi fakataha mo au 'a e Hou'eiki mo e kakai 'o Tongá pea mo e kakai Muli 'oku nofo 'i Tongá ni, 'i he me'a fakamamahi lahi kuo hokó ni 'a ia ko e Hala 'a 'Ene 'Afio ko Kuini Sālote Tupou III, pea na'e hoko ia 'i he taimi 12.15 pongipongi 'o 'e 'aho 16 'o Tīsema, 1965, 'i 'Aokalani, Nu'u Sila.

Kuo tu'utu'uni au ke fakahā 'e tauanga'a 'a Tongá ni fe'unga mo e mahina 'e ono, ko e fakahā 'o e 'ofa mo e faka'apa'apa ki he 'Ene 'Afio kuo halá 'a ia na'e pele'aki 'e he Kakai kotoa pē.

MAHE 'ULI'ULI TUPOUNIUA,
Palēmia Le'ole'o.

'Ofisi 'o e Palēmiá,
Nuku'alofa,
16 Tīsema, 1965.

16/248

FANONGONONGO

'I he Huafa 'o 'Ene 'Afio ko
TAUFA'AHAU TUPOU IV
Ko e Tu'i 'o e 'Otu Tongá

'Ia Mahe 'Uli'uli Tupouniua
Palēmia Le'ole'o 'o e
Pule'anga 'o Tongá

Koe'uhi 'i he finangalo lelei 'a 'Ene 'Afio ko e 'Otua Mafimafi koe'uhi 'i he 'Ene 'alo'ofá 'o Ne ui ki he'ene fai meesí 'a 'Ene 'Afio ko Kuini Sālote Tupou III 'a ia na'e Tu'i totonu 'i he 'Otu Tongá pea 'i he 'ene halá kuo hoko ai 'a e Kalauni 'o e Pule'anga 'o e 'Otu Tongá kia Pilinisi Tupouto'a-Tungī, ko kimautolu, Mahe 'Uli'uli Tupouniua, Palēmia Le'ole'o, Ma'afu, Sea 'o e Fale Alea; Sālesi Manoa Havea, Minisitā Polisi; Afu Taumoepeau, Minisitā Ta'e Ma'u Potungāue; Vaea, Minisitā Fonua mo Mo'ui Le'ole'o; ko e kau Minisitā 'o e Fakataha Tokoni 'o e Pule'anga 'o Tongá 'oku mau kalangaekina mo fanongonongo ko Pilinisi Tupouto'a-Tungi koe'uhi kuo hala 'a 'Ene 'Afio ko Sālote Tupou, kuo hoko ia ko e Tu'i totonu 'o e Pule'anga 'o Tongá, 'a ia kuo mau 'atu kiate ia 'a e talangofua mo e faka'apa'apa pea 'oku mau kole ki he 'Otua 'a ia 'oku 'A'ana 'a e mafai ke pule 'a e ngaahi Tu'i mo e ngaahi Kuini, ke fakafonu'aki 'a e tapuaki 'a 'Ene 'Afio ko TAUFA'AHAU TUPOU IV pea ke tuku kiate ia 'a e ngaahi ta'u lahi ke ne pule kiate kitautolu.

Na'a ku tohi nima 'i Nuku'alofa
'i he 'aho 16 'o Tīsema 'i he
ta'u 'o hotau 'Eiki tahaafe
hivangeau onongofulu ma nima.

M. E. TONGA,
Kalake 'o e Fakataha Tokoni.

'E 'OTUA FAKALAKOIFIE LELEI 'A E TU'I.

NUKU'ALOFA:
Printed and published by R. S. Wallbank, Government Printer—1965

Six weeks after her last journey from Tonga, the Queen had returned to a land of total mourning.

The *Tonga Chronicle* described the journey back to Nuku'alofa:

> Following a Royal Salute by the Guard of Honour consisting of members of the Palace Guard and the Tonga Defence Force, supported by the Police Band, Her Majesty's coffin was placed aboard the hearse for the drive into Nuku'alofa.
>
> The Royal cortège drove to Nuku'alofa through an unbroken line of school children seated at either side of the main road. Behind the children throughout the entire route from the airport were the people of Tonga seated in silent homage to their beloved late Queen. For those travelling in the cortège the scene was one of high emotion as the people, with tears in their eyes paid tribute to their former Queen as her bier was returned home.
>
> The hearse, followed by His Majesty King Taufa'ahau's car and members of the Royal Family drove down the main street of Nuku'alofa as a 21-gun salute was fired from the saluting battery on the waterfront.
>
> The cortege finally entered the Palace ground where a Guard of Honour and the bearer party were drawn up in front of the Royal Chapel. The coffin was then carried into the Chapel, where Her Majesty's body lay in state until the funeral service.

From all corners of a saddened world, the messages of sympathy arrived at Nuku'alofa—from Queen Elizabeth and Queen Elizabeth the Queen Mother, from Pope Paul and President Johnson, from Queen Juliana of the Netherlands and Crown Prince Akihito of Japan, from Governor-Generals and Governors, the Secretary of State for the Colonies, Prime Ministers and Ambassadors and many more.

A light had gone from the lives of more humble folk. In Suva, a Gujerati storekeeper asked Margaret to help him. For years, he had made shoes for the Queen of Tonga. He wished to send his personal expression of sympathy to her family and people. Could she tell him what to say? Cost was no object.

He reached up to one of the higher shelves in his shop. Inside some pages of the *Fiji Times* was a prized possession—an old pair of Queen Salote's shoes which he had copied to make a new pair for her. The Queen had permitted him to keep the old shoes as a memento of his service to her.

"At least I will have a souvenir of Queen Salote to show my children," he said proudly.

And so a telegram was drafted and sent to Tonga and the fact of it perhaps meant more than some more formal messages.

25 A Queen at Rest

HALF-PAST three at the RNZAF jetty, the ADC had said. Awake at two-forty-five: shave, shower, black suit, black tie, socks, shoes. Away from the house at three-twenty, the wreath from four former Secretaries to the Government of Tonga enveloped in polythene and resting on the back seat of the car.

One of the last operational Sunderland flying boats was tied up to the pier as we arrived. Dim figures carried stores, suitcases and uniforms in plastic bags down the steps into the chill steel of the aircraft. One after another we assembled, unspeaking. The Commander of the Fiji Military Forces, the American Consul in Fiji representing his Government, the Australian Commissioner, similarly responsible, the Colonial Secretary of Fiji, the Reverend Dr. R. G. Wood, one time Queen's Chaplain and historian of Tonga. Then the Governor of Fiji, Sir Derek Jakeway with Lady Jakeway arrived in the whirl of a Government House car. "Good trip, Sir," said the Officer Commanding, as they clambered aboard in the darkness. A roar, and we were off in the blindness of the sea, bumping into the swell inside the reef.

We began to taxi in circular sweeps. "Sorry about the delay. A bit of compass trouble," a harassed Flight Sergeant announced. "How would you like your eggs, Your Excellency?"

It was no ordinary flight for any of us. There was little conversation at first. Compounding the languor induced by broken sleep was the melancholy purpose of our journey. Dr. Wood spent most of it immersed in his notes. Apart from two days a decade before, he had not been in Tonga for some thirty years. The day previously he had been asked to deliver the royal panegyric at the graveside. He bravely proposed to do so in the Tongan language. His was a *tour de force*. He spoke lucidly for forty minutes in a language he could scarcely have used for close to half his lifetime.

During the last hour, we flew into rain squalls below a patchy layer of cloud.

"Why," I asked the pilot, "do we not fly above all this at five or six thousand feet?"

He smiled. "Do you want to freeze the toes off your Governor before he reaches Nuku'alofa? We don't have any heating. The shell of the old crate is paper-thin up top."

At 800 feet we flew in through the cloud patches over the reefs and coconut palms of western Tongatapu and out over the lagoon of Nuku'alofa. With an hour added to the Fiji clock, it was already nearly nine a.m. in Tonga. It had been eight years since my last visit and memories came flooding back as I looked down. The streets were wet from the showers, but the brown grass and roadside verges showed that Tonga, like Fiji, had suffered the South Pacific-wide drought of recent months.

Mahe was at the wharf to greet Sir Derek and Lady Jakeway, as we alighted from the pilot launch. A sallow, frail figure in black, he looked a man who had borne the burden of national grief. It was the essence of Tonga that he should still have found it possible to greet us in person—an hour before the obsequies of his Queen.

Nuku'alofa—the city of love, as the tourist guides say—was wrapped in a silence so complete that it could almost be felt. Black, black, all black—the people, the Palace, the Royal Chapel, buildings, offices, and houses, draped in vestments of unrelenting mourning. Conversation only in whispers if speech could not be avoided. In Fiji, the Legislative Council had adjourned and, on behalf of its members, the Speaker had sent a message of condolence to the new King and his Queen. The Fijian chiefs, many of them Legislative Councillors and tied by kinship with the royal or noble houses of Tonga, had already arrived to present their tributes of *tabua* (whales' teeth), *tapa*, mats and food. Among them were Ratu Edward Cakobau, half-brother of Queen Salote—Tungi Fisi (the Tungi of Fiji) as the Tongans called him; his half-brother, Ratu George Cakobau, Paramount Chief of Fiji; Ratu Kamisese Mara, with the blood of Fiji and Tonga coursing in his veins; and Ratu Penaia Ganilau, whose eulogy of Queen Salote broadcast from Fiji had touched Tongan and Fijian hearts alike.

Outside the Royal Chapel, the women were already laying the mats and *tapa* for Queen Salote's last journey. Sir Derek entered and laid his wreath. Ours were the last of the countless floral tributes. There can be few who match Tongan mastery of the assembly and display of flowers. The interior of the Royal Chapel was the quintessence of Tongan decorative skill. In the far corner was the royal casket draped with the Queen's standard, *tapa* and mats. The rest was a sea of brilliant flowers. My feet sank deep in the soft mats which had been laid inches thick over the floor. Beside the coffin stood two members of the Royal Guard, heads bowed, rifles reversed.

The wreath laid, I paused and turned to leave. In the corner of the chapel, a solitary mourner, heavily veiled in black caught my eye as I passed again into the light beyond the entrance. Her last vigil had come to an end.

I looked beyond the white walls of the Palace ground. There they were: the little wooden crosses with the names of the tributary districts of Tonga—Houma, Holonga, Kolovai, ‘Eua, Ha‘afeva, and the rest. For seven days and nights, the people had been arriving in Nuku‘alofa. Across the waterways of the island kingdom, they had journeyed in canoe and cutter as their ancestors had done for generations before. With them they brought their gifts of mats, *tapa*, oil and cooked food as last tributes to ‘Ene ‘Afio ko Kuini Salote Tupou—Her Majesty Queen Salote Tupou. Throughout the nights they sat, hushed, in their assigned places without the Palace wall, for the high ritual of chiefly death—*Koe takipo.*

When a great chief dies, fires are kept burning through the darkness around the house in which the body is lying. Each light burns over a little tray of plaited coconut leaves, on which are laid parts of the stem of the plantain tree covered with a layer of special sand. Three attendants sit on three sides of the torch. One faces the direction in which the body is lying and holds the torch horizontally over the sand pointing the same way. No one sits with his back towards the body. This is rigidly *tapu.* No person may pass between the torch and the body unless he is of superior rank to the deceased. The other attendants keep the torch burning brightly by knocking away the ash which falls on to the sand. When the torch, made from the dry spathe of the coconut flower, is nearly burned out, a new one is lit to replace the old. This is then dropped on to the sand and finally extinguished. When one of the watchers grows weary or desires a change, his place is taken by another. The lights burn on until daylight when the first light is extinguished by a person in direct chiefly relationship with the deceased. It was Princess Pilolevu, second child of the new King and Queen, who performed this task each morning during the lying in state of Queen Salote.

For the same period, no food could be prepared inside the Palace itself or the grounds. Only the new King might eat in the Palace. His Majesty's food was cooked at Talakaipau—the chiefly house in the vicinity of the Palace where Queen Salote had kept her wealth of mats, *tapa* and historic royal possessions—and brought into the Palace for him. His Queen, the new Crown Prince and the other members of the Royal Family took their meals at Talakaipau.

Inside the Royal Chapel, the casket had remained sealed. Only once was it opened—to enable King Taufa'ahau, Queen Mata'aho and the other members of Queen Salote's immediate family to kiss her for the last time. I remembered how old Tongilava had described to me the lying in state of King George Tupou I when he died on the 18th February, 1893, at the age of ninety-six. Interment was delayed for some weeks, the body being embalmed in the casket by repeated applications of powder from the sandalwood tree. The wood was filed down with the sharp vertebrae of the sting-ray attached to a stick. The undertakers covered the body with the powder which they changed about every hour. The used powder was then buried in a far corner of the royal tombs.

The sovereigns of Tonga had traditionally been buried at a place called 'Uiha in Ha'apai. After the death of George Tupou I, the Premier consulted the nobles and suggested the establishment of a new royal burial ground in Nuku'alofa. After much debate, the proposal was agreed and the old King became the first sovereign to be buried in the white raised vaults at Mala'ekula.

It was not an easy decision. Tongans dislike starting a new burial ground, lest the ghosts of the few who are interred there be lonely and seek to increase their number! Empty graves are eschewed, particularly overnight, as they constitute a threat to the living. Since the rock-lined vaults of great chiefs take time to build, a stone or wooden pillow is placed inside. This is said to frustrate the endeavours of ghosts seeking to procure an inhabitant of the grave from among the living. There was an occasion long past, at the burial of a Tu'i Tonga, when a *ha'a tufunga* man was too slow in getting out of the vault and was imprisoned with his dead king. The vault could not be re-opened to release him. To have done so would have meant that it was being breached to receive the newly appointed successor of the deceased monarch. So the unhappy undertaker had to be left inside the vault to die.

He could not therefore carry out the tasks assigned to him in the ceremonies of the succeeding ten days. The story is that each morning a messenger went to the vault and reported that his duties had been discharged by another. The imprisoned undertaker cried out his thanks that this had been done and the messenger went on his way. Then there came a day when there was no response from the vault. Lawaki, the head of the *ha'a tufunga*, concluded that the man had expired and appointed a replacement.

On the *mala'e* outside the chapel, a great concourse of mourners had assembled. The black-bordered Government funeral notice listed twenty categories in the order of procession for the walk from the Palace to the royal burial ground. There were Heads of State, representatives of other Governments and armed services, Ministers of the Crown, Heads of Churches in the Pacific, Chiefs of Fiji, Samoa and Tonga, Parliamentary Representatives, Government departmental heads and many with ties of blood to the Royal House of Tonga.

The Governor-General of New Zealand represented Her Majesty Queen Elizabeth II. The Head of State and Prime Minister of Western Samoa; the Governors of Fiji and American Samoa; the Prime Minister of New Zealand and the leader of the Parliamentary Opposition—these and numerous others, many with their wives, had come to Tonga for the funeral rites of Queen Salote.

At ten a.m. the Chapel bell began to toll and the shore battery fired a sixty-five-gun salute. A bearer party of officers of the Tonga Defence Force emerged from the Chapel carrying the coffin and placed it on a great catafalque outside. This was heavy with black drapes and little tassels hung down from the sides. Then 180 men lifted the huge bier on which were seated Lawaki and his principal lieutenant, Takapu. Led by a Guard of Honour, one hundred strong, and the Police Band, the cortège moved out on to the *mala'e*, followed by Crown Prince Taufa'ahau and Prince 'Uluvalu bearing the insignia of the honours bestowed on the Queen.

King Taufa'ahau Tupou IV and Queen Halaevalu Mata'aho, wearing the great heavy mats of mourning, walked slowly behind, heads bowed. Prince Tu'ipelehake and Princess Melenaite followed, accompanied by the rest of Queen Salote's grandchildren.

At Mala'ekula, twenty thousand black-clad men, women and children, sat quietly on the grass, not stirring during the passing showers of the morning. On arrival at the tombs, the catafalque was placed by the bearers beside the grave of Queen Salote's husband who had pre-deceased her by twenty-four years. The service was led by the Rev. G. C. Harris, President of the Free Church of Tonga; and Dr. Wood delivered his outstanding eulogy. The choir sang with a restrained beauty and tenderness unsurpassed in my experience of Tongan singing.

When the service had ended, the women of the Palace encircled the entire tomb and, facing outwards, raised a screen of mats and *tapa* cloth high over their heads so that none but the undertakers might see the actual interment of the Queen. There were faces I recognised among the women—Heuifanga, mother of Queen Mata'aho and the widow of one of Salote's nobles, Ahome'e, former Governor of Vava'u; Leafa, a Samoan woman of high rank, widow of Havea Tu'iha'ateiho, Deputy Premier in my time and a man of great personal integrity.

Three hours after we had moved from the Palace, it was over. Crown Prince Taufa'ahau descended with the Queen's decorations and sat, cross-legged on a mat before his father, facing the tomb. The screens were lowered, the bier was seen to be empty, and the undertakers began to level out the last layers of white sand on top of the grave. The vault had been closed and Queen Salote lay again beside her husband. A royal salute, a volley of rifle fire, the Last Post; then the girls of the Queen Salote College came forward to place the wealth of flowers from the Chapel above the sealed vault.

We arose as the King and Queen, their faces impassive, left to return to the Palace. Slowly we came to go, haltingly, not finding the words to speak to those known so well in the past. The Queen is dead. Long live the King. There was nothing more to say.

The undertakers would receive their bounty and would be relieved from further duty. The traditional ceremonies would go on during the six months of court and national mourning. Queen Mata'aho would go to the graveside with her women every day during that time to change the *falekakala* or scaffolding of scented chiefly flowers. Every village throughout Tonga would send their share. The *kilikili* stones would be brought from the island of Tofua. The ancient ceremony of *faka-po-teau* would take place on the hundredth night after the funeral when there would be formal presentations of food, *kava* roots and decorations for the grave. The period of mourning would come to an end with the laying of the *kilikili* stones above the vault. And Tonga would rejoice at the customary installation and coronation of its new King. So it is—even in the royal heart of Polynesia.

Five days after the departure from Tonga of Queen Elizabeth and the Duke of Edinburgh, on the 20th December, 1953, Queen Salote took part in the BBC Commonwealth Christmas programme for the first and only time. She told the world what that visit had meant and would continue to mean to her and to her people.

"Now they have gone," she went on, "the afterglow is still strongly with us and will so remain in the tales that will be told in every Tongan home by our children to their children's children through the ages to come.

"On this day of days, I send from myself and the people of my island home to you in your island home every wish for God's blessing during the Christmas season and the New Year. As it is said in the Tongan language, '*Ofa* '*atu*—goodbye and love to you all."

It might have been her own epitaph: for in her words is the memory of Queen Salote which will endure with her family and people.

Glossary

"*Coconut Wireless*"	"Beach talk," gossip, rumour.
Eiki	Chief
Faikava	The customary means of social intercourse, talking and drinking round the *kava* bowl.
Faifekau	The church minister or village preacher.
Faka-po-teau	The ancient ceremony marking the hundredth night after the sovereign's decease.
Fau	The hibiscus tree.
Ha'a Tufunga	The undertakers, a class of *matapule*
Kafa	A belt of coconut fibre sinnet wrapped round the *ta'ovala*.
Kalia	The large double canoe used by the early Polynesian voyagers.
Kava	The social and ceremonial drink of the South Pacific. It is a solution of the pulp of the root of the *kava* (*piper methysticum*) plant mixed and strained in cold water. Drunk from half-coconut shells, it has a cleansing after-effect on the palate and is pleasantly thirst-quenching on a hot day. The Fijian word is *yaqona*.
Kilikili	The volcanic black stones from the island of Tofua. They are used to decorate the raised graves of high chiefs.
Koe Takipo	The nocturnal vigil of lighted fires or torches round the place where the body of a high chief is lying before burial.
Koia, mo'oni	Indeed, it is true.
Lakalaka	A rhythmical modern dance performed by men and women dancers in parallel lines.
Lali	Hollow tree trunk used as a ceremonial drum.

Smaller lali are also common. Nowadays, the Tongans often use a forty-pound biscuit tin for the more boisterous dances. Not much of it remains at the end of the performance.

Mala'e — The public green or common land of a town or village: in particular that adjoining the Palace in Nuku'alofa.

Mala'ekula — The royal burial ground, situated on one of the estates of King George Tupou I in Nuku'alofa. Nine members of the Tongan Royal Family have been buried there since 1893.

Matapule — A lesser chief.

Ma'ulu'ulu — A sitting dance performed by either men or women.

Me'etu'upaki — A traditional religious dance, the *lali* being played in early days by the Tu'i Tonga himself.

Minisita Pa'anga — Minister of Finance.

Nopele — The Nobles.

'Otuhaka — Another early dance, the music for which is chanted. It is a sitting dance for maidens of high rank.

Sekelitali — Secretary. Often applied to the holder of the post of Government Secretary.

Tabua — Whale's tooth. Its formal presentation is the most symbolic part of Fijian traditional ceremonies. This may be to mark the welcome to a chief, the launching of a canoe, the building of a house, a death, or in the beseeching of a favour.

Ta'ovala — A woven mat worn round the waist expressing humility in the presence of a person of higher rank.

Tau'olunga — A graceful dance for soloists or groups.

Tapa — The beaten bark "cloth" of the *hiapo* tree used for clothing, bedding, decoration and

	other ceremonial and domestic purposes. Designs are imprinted or stencilled by hand with earth dyes and dyes prepared from the sap of the *koka* and candlenut trees.
Tapu	Sacred or forbidden. It virtually combines both meanings.
Tu'i Ha'atakalaua	A line of temporal kings. The holder of the title "Tungi" is the sovereign head of this royal line.
Tu'i Kanokupolu	The line of temporal kings which emerged as paramount with the establishment of the Tupou dynasty. Queen Salote was therefore also Tu'i Kanokupolu.
Tu'i Tonga	The first dynasty to rule Tonga from about 950 AD—literally, "The Kings of Tonga". They were spiritual as well as temporal rulers and as they represented the gods, they were regarded as sacred. The last Tu'i Tonga became a Roman Catholic before he died in 1865, the only one of a long line to be a Christian.
Tuku'aipe	Never mind, it doesn't matter.
Vala	The ankle-length under-skirt wrapped round the waist and legs.

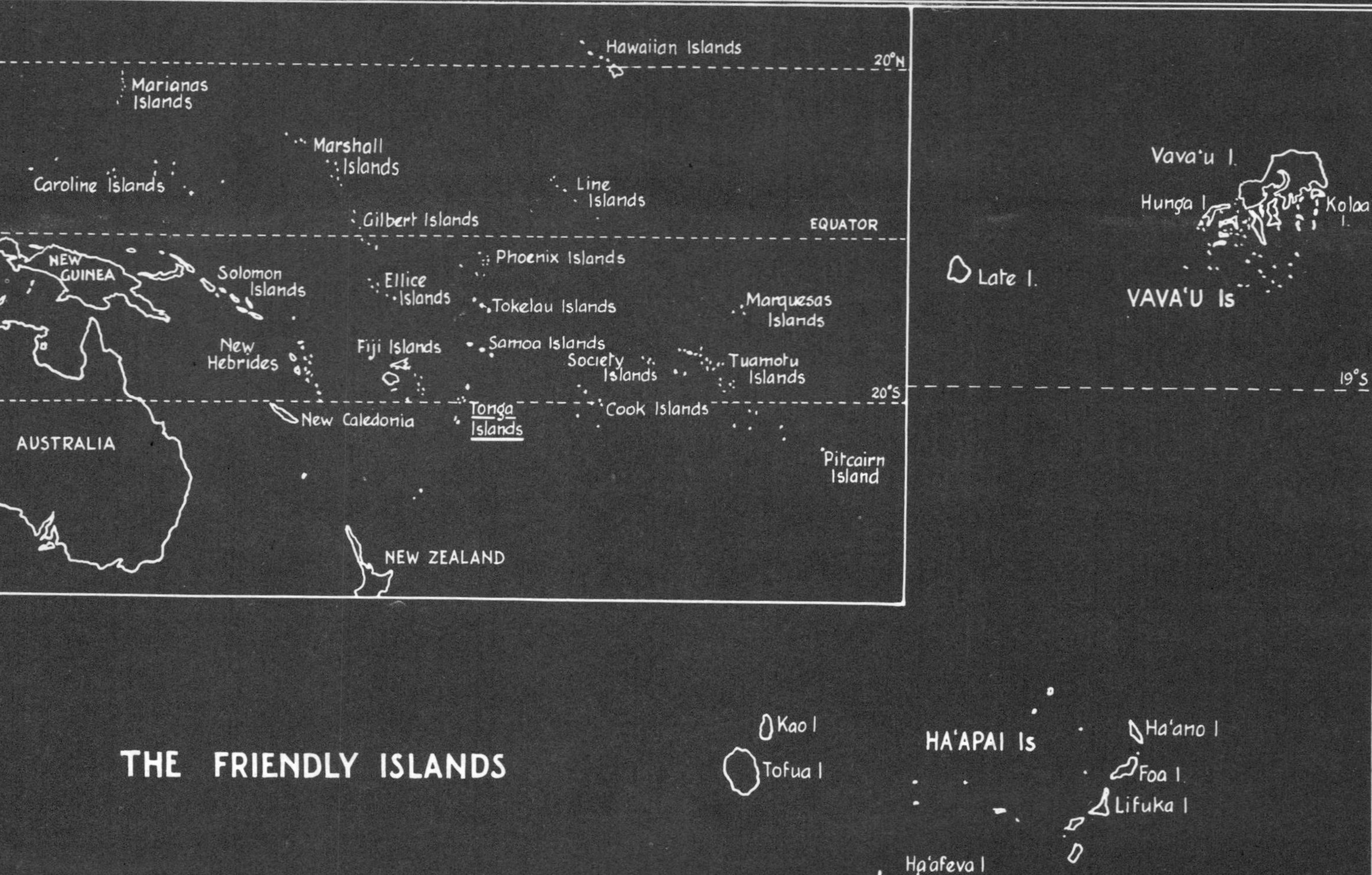
Hawaiian Islands
20°N
Marianas Islands
Marshall Islands
Caroline Islands
Line Islands
Gilbert Islands
EQUATOR
NEW GUINEA
Solomon Islands
Phoenix Islands
Ellice Islands
Tokelau Islands
Marquesas Islands
New Hebrides
Fiji Islands
Samoa Islands
Society Islands
Tuamotu Islands
20°S
New Caledonia
Tonga Islands
Cook Islands
AUSTRALIA
Pitcairn Island
NEW ZEALAND
Vava'u I.
Hunga I
Kolaa I.
Late I.
VAVA'U Is
19°S
THE FRIENDLY ISLANDS
Kao I
Tofua I
HA'APAI Is
Ha'ano I
Foa I
Lifuka I
Ha'afeva I